The Director in the Classroom

How Filmmaking Inspires Learning

Nikos Theodosakis

The Director in the Classroom
How Filmmaking Inspires Learning

Tech4Learning Publishing
San Diego, CA

For information:
Tech4Learning, Inc.
6160 Fairmount Avenue, Suite C
San Diego, CA 92120
877.834.5453 ph
619.283.8176 fax
info@tech4learning.com
www.tech4learning.com
www.pics4learning.com

Nikos Theodosakis
The Director in the Classroom
687 Main Street, Penticton
British Columbia
Canada, V2A 5C9
250.496.5348

nikos@thedirectorintheclassroom.com
www.thedirectorintheclassroom.com

Theodosakis, Nikos
  The Director in the Classroom:
How Filmmaking Inspires Learning
-1st Ed

Cover and Book Design: Sherle Raitt, R8 Design + Communications
Front Cover Photo: Matia Theodosakis by Gord Wylie
Back Cover Photo: Nikos Theodosakis by Gord Wylie
Editor: Patryce Kidd, Clearline Communications; Chandler Consulting

Printed in the United States

ISBN#: 1-930870-11-6

Passion

It was a Wednesday lunch hour at Naramata Elementary School. I was in the library with students from the grade three class helping them make their movie, *The Princess and the Street Kid.* It was a Medieval romance written by my daughter Matia and her friends and it told the story of a princess who falls in love with a poor orphan of the street. On this particular Wednesday, a student from another grade three class came in and said that she wanted to be part of this movie too. Marie was naturally athletic and has always had an incredible passion for sports, so naturally she asked if she could do something in the movie to do with sports. One of the girls in the class told her that they did not have sports in the Middle Ages, and so she could not be part of the movie. Fortunately, I was standing between them and overheard the exchange. I suggested to Marie that perhaps they did have sports and perhaps she could find out more and let the other students know for the next meeting.

The following Wednesday as I parked my car, Marie came running up to me with papers clutched tightly in hand. She erupted with excitement. "I went to the library, and I went on the Internet and I asked my dad, and they did have sports, and they had jousting and they had archery and I'm going to be William Tell!"

It was at that moment that I truly realized filmmaking's potential for enhancing students' learning experience.

My background is filmmaking, and in the last ten years I have been working with students and teachers helping them make movies in the classroom. From kindergarten to college, from documentaries to fiction, thirty-second commercials to twenty-minute dramas, I am constantly excited by what I see, and what I see is passion.

Filmmaking provides an arena where the fuel of individual passions combine to create rich, meaningful learning experiences for all students. Regardless of age, regardless of project, an engagement and eagerness for learning are unleashed when students become filmmakers. What I find fascinating about filmmaking in the classroom is how it fosters the development of a multitude of critical skills at every step of the filmmaking process.

Films begin with ideas. They evolve through brainstorming, research and discussion. In the planning stage, they require the articulation of a creative vision through written scripts, visual storyboards and oral presentations. In execution, they demand planning, organization, problem solving and maintaining focus. In editing, they require analysis, more problem solving, and the distillation and synthesis of clear, concise stories, investigations or arguments.

Filmmaking involves teams. It involves communication. It is about working towards a common goal. It is about overcoming the lack of resources and producing creative works that answer questions, reveal information and inspire. It's about seeing your work presented to an audience and your ideas communicated to others.

Within that framework, from idea to presentation, there is plenty of potential for the integration of curriculum goals, learning outcomes, higher order thinking skills, and technical learning. At the same time, the filmmaking process is all about developing awareness, creativity and self-esteem.

That is actually the part that I care about the most, guiding students through rich learning adventures and seeing them excited by the learning process and proud of their learning achievements. It is thrilling to see them beam at their own accomplishments, their eyes widened hungrily and pleading, "I want to learn more."

This is what I hope this book gives you. As well as teaching the 'how' of filmmaking, it's also about asking the important 'why?'

Why does it matter that kids enjoy the learning process?

Why does it matter that they develop team building skills, creative problem solving skills, logic skills, critical thinking skills, and research skills?

Why should they discover their community, their family and themselves?

Why is the process of learning more important today than ever before?

This book first looks at the importance of integrating filmmaking into the curriculum of today's world. It looks at the fast-changing world outside the classroom and suggests how filmmaking as a learning tool can help prepare our children for a global, visual, information-saturated, media intensive planet.

We look at how living in a visual world has led to a new visual literacy which, whether we like it or not, will increasingly surround our children and become the primary form of communication of the new millennium. We will look at how exponential change in computing, bandwidth and technology is changing how we learn and what we learn, both inside and outside the classroom walls. We will also look at the explosive growth of knowledge itself and how it reminds us why we must place more importance on learning how to learn and to think critically rather than simply memorizing facts.

In the second part of this book, we will look at the filmmaking process itself and how it inspires learning in the classroom. We design a classroom project from scratch, then follow it step-by-step through planning, production, editing and presentation. At every stage, we pause to examine some of the additional learning opportunities that are embedded in filmmaking as well as drawing connections to skill development, and issues of awareness, creativity and self-esteem.

From the beginning, we integrate curriculum objectives into video projects and then suggest assessment strategies on how to use standards and learning outcomes themselves to design the video assessment tools.

In Part Three we look at some of the real and perceived obstacles related to filmmaking in the classroom and consider them as opportunities. These include assessment of video projects, copyright issues, legal and other issues, as well as how filmmaking relates to the goals set out in the SCANS Report (Secretary's Commission on Achieving Necessary Skills).

Part Four examines how teachers themselves have the potential to be inspiring directors in their classrooms.

I wanted to create a resource book that was something between a detailed practical technical manual and an enchanting campfire story.

I believe you are holding both in your hands.

What is learning without adventure? What is adventure without tools of discovery? They go together, and each needs the other to reach its full potential.

I hope you find *The Director in the Classroom* more than a step-by-step guide on how students can create video projects. I hope you see it as a celebration of learning itself.

By looking at the successes that have already occurred in this fairly new area of teaching and learning, we can find encouragement to try more, experiment boldly and allow ourselves to be pleasantly surprised at the imagination and capabilities of our students.

The *Director in the Classroom* has been created to assist educators who have accepted the challenge to integrate filmmaking into their teaching resource kit by providing tools, processes and ideas. If you are excited by the potential of fun, engaging, project-based learning, then all you need to get started filmmaking is in this book.

The fact that you are reading this book is proof that you consider new ideas for teaching and learning, that you are on the cutting edge of making learning more relevant and engaging, that despite the obstacles of limited time, resources and education politics, that in the end, something inside you makes you go an extra mile on behalf of the learners that you guide.

This makes you an exceptional teacher, and I applaud your passion.

About the Word 'Filmmaking'

There are many ways to describe the production of movies. Some are rooted in history and others have recently surfaced in our digital age as an attempt to bridge the gap between film, video and now digital media that are used to communicate ideas visually.

Here are a few of them:

- Filmmaking
- Moviemaking
- Film production
- Video making
- Videography
- Video production
- Digital filmmaking
- Desktop filmmaking
- Digital moviemaking
- Desktop movies

I have chosen to use the word 'filmmaking' in this book, even though we are living in a digital age, for two reasons. First, the 'film' part because of the history of the word, and the 'making' because I want this book to focus on the process, the construction of visual storytelling, rather than on the technology that makes it possible.

Filmmaking reminds us that as filmmakers, we are part of a long tradition of visual story-tellers. From the late 1800s, artists, thinkers, innovators, world leaders and amateur film enthusiasts have communicated their ideas by recording images, arranging them in their pre-ferred order, and projecting them to audiences.

Their works helped influence the world of the 20th century. Dictators used the power of film to inspire their subjects. Revolutionaries used film to foster uprisings. Passionate activists used film to inform world audiences about injustices occurring all over the planet. Filmmakers of the past recorded their world so that others could learn and so that change would happen. These lessons from history have been immortalized through the hard work, persecution, creativity and perseverance of filmmakers.

As filmmakers today, students and teachers can harness the ease of use, the low cost and the speedy editing process that digital video recording equipment can offer, but I believe it is this very accessibility to a powerful medium that brings with it a responsibility to use it to its full potential.

I use the word 'filmmaker' when I talk about students creating videos because I would like them to realize that like the long line of filmmakers before them, their ideas matter.

From as early an age as possible, I want student filmmakers to realize that they too can affect change in their communities and in their world.

Thanks!

Filmmaking is a collaborative art, requiring dozens of passionate craftspeople to bring about a focused vision onto the screen. Each brings with them their own experiences and insights and makes the final film richer and truer than the director originally imagined. Writing this book was like making a film. It required artists, technicians, family and friends to join in the exploration of filmmaking in the classroom, and their experiences and insights enriched both the book and my life.

This fascinating journey began as a result of my work with educational futurist Ian Jukes. He opened my eyes to the challenges and opportunities that face education today and encouraged me to explore how my own passion for filmmaking could help address some of those challenges. Further, as a friend, he has challenged me to grow and to aim very high, and for that I thank him. I also want to thank Anita Dosaj, Bruce Macdonald and all the other Committed Sardines for their ideas and suggestions on teaching and learning in the 21st century.

Ideas need opportunities for exposure. I must thank Barry Underwood of Apple Canada for being the first person in the world to present The Director in the Classroom workshop one unassuming day in Penticton, British Columbia. As well, Mark Lewis of the Mac Doctor for providing outrageous service and support at my workshops and presentations; Lee Crockett at Shadowfax Communications for ideas, posters and graphical know how; Gary McDougall of Video Innovations for high-calibre video production and editing expertise; and the talented Gord Wylie, photographer extraordinaire who is always open to trying out ideas and always delivering fabulous images.

I had an extraordinary teacher in sixth grade named Carollyne Lansel who introduced our class to project-based learning, collaborative experiences and true adventures of investigation. She was also the first person to introduce me to a video camera and my life hasn't been the same since. My daughter Matia is now one of her students, and it has been a wonderful experience, these recent years, to step back into Carolyn's classroom. Thank you to all the teachers that shared their stories of classroom filmmaking struggles and successes, especially to Marco Torres, Don Henderson, Cherrie Hansen and Tammy Kay.

Thanks to writer Randy Bartel who was one of the first to lend an ear and help translate rambling explorations into focused ideas. And thanks to Cherrie Hansen and Anne Marie Thorslund, who tried to teach me a few things about 'speling and grammarage,' but failed due to my love of saying things wrongly.

Big thanks to Cynthia Chandler for introducing me to the Tech4Learning Group. David Wagner and Melinda Kolk of Tech4Learning have core values and goals beautifully aligned with the intent of *The Director in the Classroom*. Their products champion creativity in the classroom and their company pulsates with a passion for learning. I am proud and excited to be launching this book under their flag. I also want to thank Cynthia for having faith in these ideas and in myself enough to introduce both to school districts and conferences around the United States. As well, I thank her for the input and feedback that helped shaped the final content of this book.

Thanks to Sherle Raitt for taking hundreds of emails full of quotes, chapters, forms and ideas and turning them into the book that you are holding. And besides the technical wizardry, thank you Sherle for the many creative conspiracies over the years.

Thanks to Sandy Wilson who gave me my introduction into filmmaking and introduced me to the world of directing. Thanks to Mort Ransen who enabled me to study more about directing through an apprenticeship and who insisted that I go out and learn more. Thanks to Judy Weston for teaching me that 'more'—about directing, about acting and about how great teachers teach.

Thanks to Martin Fossum and Franco Pante, filmmakers and dear friends, who have made my journey into filmmaking rich with passion. Thanks to Steve Denure, who taught me how great producers inspire their teams, and to Dianne Neufeld who encouraged me to inspire others.

Thanks to the aunts and uncles who said, "Go for it!" Sophie, Larry, Chris, Janice and Kosta. Thanks to my grandfather Gergio who told me once, "σαν ενε ο τραγοξ δινατοσ, θεν τον κρατα το μαδρα, ο ανδρασ κανι τι γενια, και οχι τι γενια τον ανδρα."

Thanks to my father who taught me how to look at the world as a producer—creating buildings from barren lots, and businesses from brave ideas and indefatigable drive. Thanks to my mother who taught me how to look at the world as a director—through questioning eyes, creative investigation and spiritual compassion. Synthesis was inevitable and invaluable.

Thank you Sophia for waltzing into my office each day, demanding, "Baba, dance with me!" and reminding me to invite dance and love into each day. Thank you Matia, for inviting me to help you and your friends make a movie at Naramata School and inspiring me to create *The Director in the Classroom*. I love the way your mind works.

Linda, thank you for your nourishing, assiduous, multifarious love and for teaching me how to listen, observe and ask questions. This book is dedicated to you.

Thank you.

Nikos Theodosakis
Naramata, British Columbia
Canada, 2001

Foreword

Do you remember back to a time when virtually all of our information was paper-based information? We learned left-to-right, top-to-bottom, beginning-to-end, linear-logical-sequential.

Today, children not only have to learn left-to-right, top-to-bottom, beginning-to-end, but they are also expected to be able to communicate with pictures and sounds as well as they do with words and sentences. They are expected to be able to understand and utilize graphic designs and video as well as they do the linear, logical left-to-right, top-to-bottom text based world that we come from.

As Jason Ohler writes in his marvelous new book *Taming the Beast*, we have moved from the 3Rs to the 4Rs. From Reading, Writing and Rithmetic, to Reading, Writing, Rithmetic and Art. Art has become the next great literacy.

This is where Nikos' book comes in.

This book looks at the potential of using digital video in the classroom as a powerful tool for teaching and learning. It explores how filmmaking in the classroom prepares students for living in a digital, visual, information saturated 21st century.

This book talks about the real issues of education. These are issues that have little to do with hardware and software, or cards and cables. This book is about moving beyond LOTS (Lower Order Thinking Skills with LOTS of information) approach to a HOTS (Higher Order Thinking Skills) approach to the use of powerful technologies. This book is about how to use powerful technologies such as digital video to embed critical learning experiences into the classroom.

This book is about helping children to move beyond simple content recall and the traditional basics to the new basics. This book is about effective strategies that will allow our children to become critical thinkers, problem solvers, decision-makers, effective time managers and visually literate.

This is a remarkable book written by a unique man. Someone with a deep understanding of the technical issues combined with a clear understanding of the critical skills, knowledge and understandings necessary to live and learn in a digital age. This book you hold contains some simple yet powerful ideas.

Nikos has provided a detailed map to take us from where education is to where it needs to be. It's not the only map by any means, but a compelling map as to how we can help transform an aging and increasingly irrelevant institution into something that will have real meaning and relevance to the lives of this and future generations. Therefore, the challenge is up to you. How will you use this map? What will you see and how will you respond when you gaze at the world that stands in front of us? Most important, what concrete actions will you take as a result of reading this book?

As you journey across the terrain called education, heed the words of Helen Keller: "The only thing worse than not being able to see, is being able to see and having no vision."

Ian Jukes, September, 2001

Table of Contents

Part 1: Why Filmmaking Belongs in the Classroom

Part 2: The Filmmaking Process in the Classroom

Part 3: Obstacles are Opportunities

Part 4: Teachers as Directors

Part 5: Appendix

Part 1:

Why Filmmaking Belongs in the Classroom

"I think the big mistake in schools is trying to teach children anything, and by using fear as the basic motivation. Fear of getting failing grades, fear of not staying with your class, etc. Interest can produce learning on a scale compared to fear as a nuclear explosion to a firecracker."
Stanley Kubrick

1. Living and Learning in a World of Change

Learning in a World of Change

We are living in a world of constant change. Computer technology and specifically the Internet have changed forever the way we live, the way we work and the way we learn. Information is the new commodity and resource of communities, corporations and countries. Knowledge is being shared, exchanged, bought and sold and created at a rapidly increasing pace. In the middle of all this change are our children who we as adults, parents and educators try to guide in their navigation and understanding of this bombardment of information.

As a parent, I find myself trying to prepare my children for their future based on what I know about the world that I see around me balanced with what changes I think will transpire in the years ahead. As I try to create a path for learning, I am constantly trying to determine the direction that path should take. The problem is, like everything else around me, the direction keeps changing.

Just when I think I have it figured out, new technologies come along and radically change the way things are done or significantly alter the ideas and concepts of the world around me. Understandably, I feel that society just can't keep up with all the changes and new information imposed upon it. But far from being hopeless, it is actually a mixed blessing.

What this constant change and overload of information makes us realize is that we must change our own attitudes and our assumptions of not only what we teach our children, but also how we teach them. Because they will exist in a world of even more exponential and constant change than we now know, we must do our best to prepare them for being citizens who understand the learning process itself.

They must be able to know where to find the information they need when they need it, to know how to process that information,

"Look let's face it, the cinema—the classical cinema—is gone. It's over. The cinema as we know it up to now, is disappearing. It doesn't mean that cinema is dead. Rather, it's evolving. It's new, totally new. So new, that some of us may not even be aware of what changes will occur in the next decade."
Martin Scorcese

"All television ever did was shrink the demand for ordinary movies. The demand for extraordinary movies increased. If any one thing is wrong with the movie industry today, it is the unrelenting effort to astonish."
Clive James

and then to know how to present their ideas to their families, communities, audiences, work mates and business associates. The need becomes apparent. We should focus on helping our children develop research, communication, problem solving, and other higher order thinking skills that will benefit them for the rest of their lives.

Why Content is Not What it Used to Be

My daughter Matia is nine years old and my youngest daughter Sophia is five. A question in the forefront of my mind is, "What will they have to learn over the next twelve to sixteen years of their formal education to prepare them for the world that they will influence and be influenced by?"

The Law of Technological Information[1] maintains that the amount of technological information doubles every eighteen months. This means that by the time Sophia finishes her fourth year of college, there will be approximately 1024 times the amount of technological information that there is today.

Content is not what it used to be.

These are not the days that my grandparents or parents experienced where the content they learned in classrooms (or from their parents or mentors) was enough to prepare them for a life-long career.

According to a Department of Education report[2], the graduating class ten years from now will be working in jobs and careers that have yet to be invented. They will use technologies that do not yet exist to solve problems that have yet to be imagined.

This scares me, but also reminds me that we have to ask ourselves questions. How, why and what do we teach?

The days of memorizing information and being able to recall it later may have served my generation, or the generation of my parents and grandparents, but memorization alone will not help Sophia. What is needed is a balance between the understanding

1. Telecosm : How Infinite Bandwidth Will Revolutionize Our World by George Gilder, 2000

2. Richard Riley, the then secretary of education in a February 1999 speech at the KETC in Louisville, KY.

of language, mathematics, science, social studies, and other curriculum with the ability to learn how to learn. This is why any learning that contributes to the development of process skills serves learners twice. First, as a way to understand the content that exists in their world today, and second, as a way to explore, develop, and understand the learning processes that they will require forever.

Process is Forever

We have all heard the parable, "Give a man a fish, he eats for one day, teach him to fish, and he eats forever." Granted, it may be a bit overused, but its message is clear: process is forever.

Tell students that the capital of Greece is Athens and ask them to memorize it until test day and they just might. Hand out lists of facts about Greece and ask them to memorize them as well, and perhaps most of those could also be remembered. The question is, "How long will it be remembered, and what will they have really gained through the process of memorization?"

But consider a project-based learning approach where students discover their knowledge. Announce to students that you have become the owner of International Travel Network and they have become television producers. Invite proposals from filmmaking teams of four or five students to each submit a proposal for a travel video that would introduce your television audience to the highlights of a trip to Athens.

- What things should travelers know about going to Athens?
- What attractions would they record? Why?
- How do you get around in Athens?
- What kind of music might be playing in the background?
- What language do people speak?
- What is there to do at night?
- What's on the menu at favorite restaurants?
- What cultural activities occur this time of year?

- What should travelers wear? Is it hot?
- How would they get to Athens from here?

Now send them to libraries, web sites, travel agents, and Greek restaurants and let them uncover the content related to the learning. The proposals will be rich and the information on the pages earned.

I love reports and presentations that are developed in this way because they are all about discovery. When we learn by discovery, something happens. The brain wakes up and takes notice. Information is processed into knowledge.

This is the important role that we have to remember: to give students avenues of discovery and to guide them towards the uncovering of that information so that they will not only gain a long-term understanding of the content that is being explored, but so that they also develop skills in discovering new knowledge.

In a report entitled The Impact of Media and Technology in Schools (1998), a research report prepared for The Bertelsmann Foundation by Thomas C. Reeves, PhD of the University of Georgia describes the results of an interesting experiment in learning by R. Lehrer. The full document can be viewed at <*www. athensacademy.org/instruct/media_tech/reeves0.html*>.

He explains how two groups of eighth graders studied the American Civil War. One group, called the control group, was instructed via traditional classroom practices. The other group, called the design group, worked on constructing multimedia projects for one class period of forty-five minutes each day over a period of several months. The students constructed their projects in the school's media centre that had a colour computer, scanner, sound digitizer, HyperAuthor™ software and numerous print and non-print resources. There was an instructor available to help students conceptualize, design and construct their projects.

Students created multimedia reports reflecting their own interests. Some explored the role of women in the American Civil War, others explored the war from the slaves' perspectives, and others

examined the war from the perspective of "not-so-famous people."
According to Lehrer[3], "The most striking finding was the degree
of student involvement and engagement."

At the end of the study, both groups were given an identical
teacher-constructed test of knowledge and guess what happened?

"No significant test differences were found."

When I read this, I was very surprised. I thought that the design
group would score higher because of the richer learning experience.
Reading further, it was revealed that one year later, an independent
researcher tested students from both groups. He found that the
students in the control group, "…could recall almost nothing
about the historical content, whereas students in the design group
displayed elaborate concepts and ideas that they had extended to
other areas of history."

Although students in the control group defined history as,
"…the record of the facts of the past," students in the design class
defined   history as "a process of interpreting the past from different perspectives." In short, "the design approach led to knowledge
that was richer, better connected, and more applicable to subsequent learning and events."

Subsequent learning is the key phrase for me because it
assumes, rightly so, that learning will continue. It affirms that the
process of investigating information through discovery rather than
memorization has life-long benefits to our students. By giving
students tools for discovery we are equipping them for learning
throughout their classroom years and beyond, into the rest of their
lives.

My wife Linda told me that when she heard of this report,
it was as if the control group were, "…plants without roots that
looked good for a while but fell over in time and that the design
group had developed roots that went deep into the ground. Those
roots not only helped the ideas to survive over time, but were able
to nurture the ongoing blossoming of new ideas."

*"We're witnessing a new
cinema being born and
that's exciting. However,
whatever cinema evolves
into, you still need an
author."*
Martin Scorcese

[3.] Section 3: The Impact of Learning
'With' Media and Technology in
Schools; Research Results.

2: Living and Learning in a Visual World

Living in a Visual World

Now more than ever, we are living in a visual world. We take for granted that television, movies, magazines, and billboards exist to sell us ideas using images. And with the introduction of the World Wide Web and the latest digital technologies, we have seen even more uses of visual communication.

It was not long ago that web sites were primarily text-based with perhaps a static image or two. Today, we witness multimedia web sites that compete visually for our attention and patronage.

Even email is taking on a new look. I was amazed the first time I received an email with a photo attachment and I shook my head when I received my first video attachment. It makes me wonder how we will see images become even more a part of our day-to-day lives.

As technologies develop will we see web sites delivered on full screen video walls in our homes? Will we receive holograms on our desks? What about virtual reality experiences at the local cinema or in our living rooms?

Last week Linda and I took our daughters to a play centre where they skied down virtual slopes on real skis, paddled real oars up a virtual river, and wore Virtual Reality goggles to experience a hang gliding adventure. On the same weekend, we took them to an IMAX film where gigantic images of the sun and the solar system widened their eyes.

Although we do not know the details of tomorrow's technology, we can speculate that we will witness an increased use of visual imagery to convey information, to advertise, to entertain, and to share and stimulate ideas.

"We live in a time where things do not seem to exist unless they have been captured in an image."
Peter Mettler

Learning in a Visual World

If we expect our children to be both consumers and producers of visually communicated ideas, we have to ask ourselves, "How do we prepare them for that visual world?" If we expect them to be fluent in this new visual language, where do we begin teaching the visual grammar and visual vocabulary skills that will help them both understand and present concepts and ideas that use images as well as or instead of text?

One option is an early integration of visual communication experiences into the learning process. We need to let them practice and learn though personal experiments with visual communication projects. We are familiar with traditional art instruction such as drawing, painting, photography and design. Increasingly, we see the proliferation of courses that teach video editing, web page construction, CD-ROM, DVD creation and other new technologies.

What is often missing, and this has been a major concern for the last decade, is exactly how those new technologies are being taught. Too often, it is about teaching students how to 'do' a spreadsheet, a web page, or how to edit a video. What is needed is the continual asking of the question, "How can these new technologies empower our students to be better communicators of their ideas?"

Learning the technology is not enough. What is really required is learning how to use that technology to solve problems, to answer questions, to present ideas, and to communicate.

We know that new technologies will always be on the horizon, and that they will augment or replace what is being used today.

While the "content" of the technology that is being taught may be obsolete in a few years, the process of its use as a tool for learning and its purpose for communicating ideas will have long-lasting applications.

When I first began working with video twenty years ago using half-inch open reel video technology, we would wind up the tape onto reels, spool it through, put a cover on the deck, and then attach an umbilical cord to a mega-sized black and white camera in order to go out and record.

When we edited, we would find our edit points by dragging the tape across the play head; then, holding onto the right reel, we'd unspool the left reel until the videotape touched the floor. Then we would wind up both decks and let them play. We would look back and forth between the two monitors and if it looked like it might work, we pressed the record button and hoped for the best.

Although I can laugh at the now obsolete technology that I used, the skills that I learned as a story teller and a communicator have stayed with me to this day.

It is hard for us to imagine that today's digital non-linear editing systems will seem archaic and even laughable twenty years from now, but this is the course that technology innovation is on. Because of this, we cannot get hung up on the technological tools themselves; we must instead focus on what these tools can bring to learning.

In the next chapter, we examine specifically how filmmaking using today's technology of digital video helps develop multiple critical skills for our students which will serve them for years to come.

"Actually, film operates on a level much closer to music and to painting than to the printed word, and, of course, movies present the opportunity to convey complex concepts and abstractions without the traditional reliance on words. I think that 2001, like music, succeeds in short-circuiting the rigid surface cultural blocks that shackle our consciousness to narrowly limited areas of experience and is able to cut directly through to areas of emotional comprehension. In two hours and forty minutes of film there are only forty minutes of dialogue."
Stanley Kubrick

3: How Filmmaking Develops Higher Order Thinking Skills

In this chapter, we look at some of the ways that filmmaking helps develop higher order thinking skills. The filmmaking process in the classroom invites a variety of skills to be explored and developed as the students journey from the creation of the original idea to the first presentation and beyond.

Visioning Skills

Filmmaking is about turning the intangible into the tangible. Regardless of the size of the film, whether it's *Ben Hur* or *My Science Experiment*, movies start with that wonderful thing called "the idea." As the idea formulates in the mind of the filmmaker, a vision of the final film begins to develop. When the idea becomes a script, the challenge for directors is to hold a clear picture in their minds of what they want to communicate and then to guide their crew towards that vision. The goal of the filmmaking process and all involved is to put that vision on the screen.

When students create a film, it is an opportunity for them to develop a vision of what they want to explore and to see how the vision changes or remains the same as they set out and make it happen. It is practice in turning the intangible into the tangible.

It's also about learning the process of looking at where you want to be, looking at where you are now, and constructing a plan to connect the two. The skill of working backwards from a goal, and translating it into a plan of action, can be transplanted for personal achievement in many fields.

It can also lead into a discussion of what 'vision' itself is, as filmmakers telling stories, as teams of people following a common goal or as individuals pursuing a dream.

It's about exploring not only what the vision is, but also what the vision does. How it moves you into action, gets you up on your feet, makes you advance in order to crystallize what you have in your mind.

It is important that students develop visioning skills for both their present and future worlds. We need students to see how ideas can be transformed into action and how if they want to reach for something, if they can dream it, they can do it. But for them to realize the dream, the idea, the target, it begins with being able to articulate clearly the vision they hold in their minds to themselves and to others.

Films get made because a vision can be imagined, articulated, realized and shared. If we believe that students would benefit from this entrepreneurial approach to learning, then this is another benefit that filmmaking gives them.

Research

When audiences go to see a film in the theatre, they seldom realize how much research goes into the making of the movie. The filmmaking process uses extensive research throughout. In the formative stages, writers, directors and producers research story ideas that relate to the idea they are imagining. They interview people, read books, clip magazine articles, scan the Web, draw upon personal experiences and look to uncover information from anywhere they can, knowing that key secrets can be revealed in the least likely of places.

Once an idea is decided upon, the writer will usually research as much material as they can find in order to get a better understanding of the context and content of the story.

My wife, Linda, is a writer. One of the characters in her latest screenplay works with autistic adults. Linda has been researching autism on the Web, interviewing caregivers who work with autistic adults, and has arranged to work-shadow some of these caregivers and their clients. The more she researches, the more it informs her story. The more facts and truths that she uncovers, the better the possibility that the story will ring true to her audience.

As a director, I also conduct research as I endeavor to become familiar with the story and setting of the project that I have undertaken. I research story facts, location characteristics, design elements, themes, characters and many other components.

In addition, our cameraman (man or woman camera operator) might research lighting, colour, design and visual styles for his or her subject, perhaps choosing to contrast harsh institutional lighting in some scenes with warm comforting tones in another.

The production manager will research what resources are available at the location where the film is to be recorded. He or she will investigate where to rent equipment, vehicles, facilities and where to hire local cast and crew.

There is an exhaustive amount of invisible research undertaken by almost all the members of the creative and production crew. Because there is so much investigation embedded in the filmmaking process, it fosters the development of research skills as students prepare and produce their own videos. As information exponentially explodes all around us, the ability to effectively mine that information also increases.

If we are to prepare students to make sense of all that information, then familiarization with good research skills— knowing where to find things, how to find things, who to ask, how to collect it and how to organize it—becomes another important skill developed by filmmaking.

Problem Solving Skills

Filmmaking is problem solving. Turning the vision in the creator's mind into the finished movie on screen requires a seemingly endless journey into problem solving, not only in terms of what do we want to show, but also, how we will show it.

Regardless of budget, filmmakers always come up against obstacles in filming. It could be that the actor you would like is not available, or possibly you were hoping for a sunny day but it

"Some of these big American films get made in this very efficient way, where a script is written by a scriptwriter and the director comes in and makes his comments, gets a storyboard artist to draw the thing up, and he hires a designer who designs it, a costumer comes in to do the costumes, and the films get made and they're fine, and they work in a system that works very well. I just try to break that down, by trying to get everyone involved in doing everything on the film. So the costumer is coming up with ideas for sets, and the set designer might be coming up with an idea for the costumes. You try to get the right team of people to feed it and then they feed you, and it goes back and forth. I think that's why there's so much detail, because people are thinking about it and the detail becomes as important as the characters in the film."
Terry Gilliam

is raining. It could be that you do not have enough money for the budget you require. It may be that you do not have the equipment you need. You might not have access to the location you wish you could shoot at. Or you may simply need more time. The list, unfortunately, is endless. But what the appearance of problems does is create a perpetual arena for problem-solving opportunities.

Since some of our greatest challenges in education today are to stretch already tight budgets, to share limited resources, and to accommodate multiple objectives within limited time constraints, there exists a great opportunity to take advantage of what these challenges offer.

In other words, as students set out to create their films and discover obstacles of time, equipment and other resources, they learn to identify and solve their own problems, and to own the process for finding solutions. It is then that these multiple, real world filmmaking challenges have become a great opportunity to experience real world problem solving.

Logic Skills

Sometimes when I am putting together a film, I feel like I'm in the middle of a giant algebraic equation. So many decisions in filmmaking are affected by so many other decisions. If this happens, then that can happen; if this does not happen, then this other thing has to happen. IF it is sunny, we will shoot Scene 16 by the lake with all the actors and props required for that scene; IF it rains, THEN we will shoot the interior scene in the cabin living room. There are so many decisions that are interwoven into so many other decisions in filmmaking. This decision-making process requires the development and utilization of good logical thinking skills. It is like playing a game of chess and imagining the impact a move now will have, six moves in the future.

In the classroom the process of filmmaking requires students to imagine what they will need to make their movie. As they are asked to develop a strategy of planning, production and editing, they start assembling a logical series of events and resources to make it all come together. Regardless of whether this process is articulated on paper, or simply considered in their minds, that process will occur.

Planning Skills

Again, one of the invisible skills that ties the filmmaking process together and allows movies to be created is the critical skill of planning and time management. Estimating how long things will take and how they will get done is extremely important to the filmmaker. Because the cost of actors, equipment and resources is so expensive, a great deal of time is spent planning when and how those elements can best be used.

In fact, the Production Department is a whole team of people on a film crew that is dedicated to planning, organizing and scheduling. The team meets with the other departments well before filming begins and examines the details of each of the production elements that are, or might be, required. Once they have investigated what resources are required, they then create a plan for its realization.

A feature film is very rarely filmed in sequential order. This is because time, money and other resources can be better utilized if similar scenes are shot at the same time. Often these scenes are grouped by location, or by actors, or by equipment availability. A richly detailed tool called the Production Board and planning documents like the scene breakdowns (a dissection of each scene that lists what actors, sets, props and other key ingredients are required for each scene), location breakdowns (a list of where the filming will take place), cast day out of days (a list of when the actors work each day) and other planning documents are used by the production team to detail the requirements of each of the scenes. In the next part of this book, we will look at them in more detail and see how they might be used in the classroom.

Filmmaking in the classroom allows students to explore their own planning and time management skills, both in terms of managing their own time and resources, as well as those of the whole group, for example their crew. The results of poor or good time management can be examined and used as another learning tool in this process.

If the students' attempt at scheduling did not meet their expectations, the feedback is immediate. This can lead into an exploration of what they would do differently on the next day of shooting or on the next project. If things took longer than they thought (a common occurrence in both professional and student filmmaking), how do we learn from that and change how we estimate and plan our time?

As with all the skills, it is, of course, intended that the students' understanding and abilities transcend video production and become useful across their whole learning and living experience. Since planning is a critical component of filmmaking and also a critical life skill, the experiences students learn in time management and planning will benefit them for all their lives.

Analytical Skills

Another skill which is invisible to the movie audience, but which is essential to the filmmaker, is the ability to critically analyze information. As a director, when I am standing on a film set, my role is to take in all the information about the scene that I have researched, or experimented with, and all the new information that I am receiving from the actors, the crew or the location, and analyze it against my vision for that particular scene. It is about looking at all the information and deciding what should be included and what should be left out. It is about 'filtering' information on your feet.

Later, during the editing process, I will look at multiple takes of the same shots, and multiple shots of the same scene, and decide, after I look at all of this information, which film footage best illustrates what I am trying to communicate and what I want to explore. As long as we continue to be overloaded with information and continual decision making, the development of analytical processes will be an important survival skill for students.

Although there is a lot of information on the Internet, in libraries, in books, in magazines and in conversation with the people all around us, it is best turned into knowledge by students when it is gathered, analyzed, and represented in accordance with their points of view. Because students must analyze information in order to produce their individual videos, we create opportunities to exercise this critical skill.

"I feel, a lot of times, like I'm a football player and the football is the movie. And on that field, with all those people running interference to me—studio executives, managers, agents, publicists, critics, journalists—I'm just trying to get the ball past the goal line and into the stands to the audience. Sometimes it's very pleasant, sometimes it's an obstacle course."
Joel Schumacher

4: How Filmmaking Develops Personal and Social Skills

Along with the development of higher order thinking skills, the filmmaking process enables students to experience and develop personal and social skills. The process of creating and the satisfaction of completing any project, not only a filmmaking project, helps build creativity, confidence and self-esteem. The completion of a creative product teaches students that they can achieve and empowers them to reach higher. The act of acquiring the knowledge through the construction of the project not only creates an understanding of the topic being covered but also has the added benefit of fostering intangible, un-testable personal and social skills.

Creativity

Filmmaking is about creativity. It is about looking at a question and approaching it, exploring it, investigating it from different perspectives and different points of view. These points of view are informed and influenced by each filmmaker's upbringing, interest and personal battles. The people they know and the events they have experienced also help them form their concepts.

In short, their life experiences and individual perspectives conspire to fabricate their own unique approach to investigating and communicating the subject.

Filmmaking provides students with the opportunity to explore the creative process. It affords them first-hand experience from original inspiration to completion of the final product and fosters personal discoveries of their own approach to the creative process. The approach to the subject itself is a great example of how students are able to develop their creativity.

For example, a project may be designed with the purpose of raising awareness of the art and culture that exists in a community. The specific goal may be to create a video document about an artist that lives in the community.

"I wrote in an Italian newspaper when he died that the world without Fellini was for me as if olive oil was dead. Fellini and Bunuel changed my life for me, they are my favourites. If it is true that movies are dreams, both of them, Fellini and Bunuel were shooting in a dream way. I don't know what gift the sky gave to them, but they shot in the dream way, in the style of dreams. I am grateful to them, because now the world looks different to me."
Roberto Benigni

Now some students are going to interview painters and potters. Some will approach musicians or dancers. Others may decide on a tattoo engraver, a performance artist, or their kid brother's bedroom murals created with the medium of chocolate pudding. The interpretation of the question itself is fascinating. By providing loose project criteria, we provide students opportunities to create their own avenues of exploration defined by their own interest, inquiry and creativity.

Filmmaking is a creative medium comprised of many artists and craftspeople working together, each bringing their own approach to the project while at the same time working towards the common goal. For students, this is about having the freedom to work through projects in their own style, but at the same time working within the framework of what needs to be done.

In addition to filmmaking being about how creativity is used in aesthetic choices, it is also about how it is used in logistical choices. Filmmaking is creative problem solving. It is a continual process of identifying obstacles (e.g. not enough money, time, resources) and setting out to overcome them through creative problem solving. Filmmakers of all ages overcome barriers by looking at different possibilities and identifying which possible solutions exist and which are worth exploring.

Every single day, on film sets around the world, filmmakers, camera operators, lighting technicians, sound engineers, actors, art directors, and in fact every single craftsperson, bring their own creativity to identify challenges, create solutions and enhance their production.

I once worked on a film where the lighting technician on the film crew told me proudly of an obstacle that he had overcome. A movie was being photographed in the interior of an old bank building that had a five-story open lobby. The director of photography required a wall of even light to be streaming into the vast space to light the set.

"A different language is a different vision of life."
Federico Fellini

The choreographed action of the actors and the constant movement of the camera prevented the gaffer from placing lights on lighting stands, as he would normally do in this situation. He had to light from above without having anything to put lights on. There were no balconies or levels, only straight, sheer walls. As well, the director of photography wanted to control the level of light and be able to change it as actors moved closer to the camera.

The gaffer thought of this problem for many days and eventually came up with an idea. He decided he would point lights from the floor, hidden from the camera, onto a huge white tarp suspended in mid air with large helium filled weather balloons hovering above. He secured them with guide wires and constructed a pulley system whereby he could increase or decrease the illumination on the set by lowering or raising the helium balloons and thus the tarp. Further, he could angle the tarp on just one corner to allow for more precise lighting. His solution worked, the film was shot, and long after the film has been forgotten, he still entertains people with his stories of how he found a creative solution to his problem.

In the classroom, I see students using wheelchairs as dollies, putting cameras on skateboards to get low angles and inventing all kinds of camera cranes, mounts and devices to get their shots. If necessity is the mother of invention, filmmaking is the father.

Confidence and Self Esteem

Childhood depression is widely recognized as a major concern in the world today. Health professionals see depression as a serious condition affecting both adolescents and young children. Research suggests that major depression affects one in fifty school children. The suicide rate in teenagers has quadrupled in the last quarter century, making it the third leading cause of adolescent death in the nation.

Depression has long been tied to low self-esteem. Traditionally

"I think the big mistake in schools is trying to teach children anything, and by using fear as the basic motivation. Fear of getting failing grades, fear of not staying with your class, etc. Interest can produce learning on a scale compared to fear as a nuclear explosion to a firecracker."
Stanley Kubrick

"If you're worrying about how to finance and distribute your movies than you shouldn't bother making movies. You make movies because you need to make movies. Everything else is unimportant. If you wait to get the money to make a movie then you shouldn't make the movie. If you need distribution in place before you have the courage to make a movie then it's not a movie worth making. There are many other ways to make money than making movies. If you need to make money, please find some other way to do it. You make movies to lose your money. That is the purpose of making a movie—to put your life into something—not get something out of it."
John Cassavettes

it was thought that if one could improve the way an individual perceived himself, then the secondary behaviours that accompany low self-esteem would disappear (New model, 1995).

New research now suggests that there is a correlation between a person's emotional self-esteem and their standing in interpersonal relationships. The result of social rejection results in low self-esteem and, conversely, the perception of social success leads to improved self-esteem.

Filmmaking in the classroom provides the following opportunities to increase confidence and self-esteem:

- It provides opportunities for students to work in small groups where they can be part of a team that organizes, produces and presents their film.
- It provides opportunities to develop interpersonal relationships with others.
- It provides opportunities for success. The ability to see a project realized helps build confidence that more can be achieved.
- It provides an arena for students to present their own points of view.

But without looking at it so clinically, what I love about seeing kids picking up cameras and creating movies is their unabashed sense of self-worth. They take their work seriously and approach their subject with respect. They can sense their own confidence building and their own creativity flowing.

Students see themselves as real filmmakers, and why shouldn't they? That's what they are.

Pride of Ownership

Oh the joy of completing a film! Filmmaking is a long journey of overcoming obstacles, determination, working alone, working with others and maintaining a clear focused vision. Everyone who completes a film should receive an award just for finishing.

There is a sense of pride that manifests itself at the end of that journey, and that pride is its own reward—one's own recognition and respect for the importance and value of what they have achieved. For many, this sense of accomplishment is a catalyst for more. Recognizing that one can indeed make a film then begs the question, "What else can I do? Not only what other film can I make, but also what else can I create?"

In my experience with students, this pride can be summed up in two words. They beam! How else can you describe that ear-to-ear grin, the shy smiles and the confessions of having 'fun'? Projects that go outside the classroom give students the satisfaction that people in their community and possibly around the world will see what they have created.

I really enjoy hearing the stories of classroom filmmaking, stories about what obstacles were in the way and how the students overcame the problems. I love the way students own the process from start to finish and how those stories linger on, becoming their own mythologies months after the film is completed.

Most importantly, the ability to make meaning out of solving a problem brings with it a deep construction of the knowledge itself.

Individuality

Imagine an assignment where everyone in the class is asked to create a short video on the same topic. How many different videos will be produced? Probably as many different kinds of videos as there are students. Why? Because everyone is going to bring something different to the project, approach it with a slightly different perspective, or record it with a different lens, a different angle, or make distinct editing choices. What better way to start talking about how being different is not only natural, but also necessary for our society?

Filmmakers make films differently from one another. This is not

"Make visible what, without you, might perhaps never have been seen."
Robert Bresson

a bad thing. To be unique is good. To have a personal perspective is wonderful. In filmmaking, individuality and uniqueness are expected. How we each approach problem solving and how we each approach the filmmaking process, in general, are reflections of our own singularity. What I want to celebrate is that filmmaking is a personal process. It is a reflection of who we are.

Passion

In this world where measuring one's knowledge has become so important, we don't have a test for one of the most critical traits that we can possess: Passion. And this is sad because it is passion that drives the exploration that drives the investigation that becomes the knowledge.

It is the passion of the filmmakers that drives the project, and allows them to endure ridicule, obstacles and fatigue in the name of getting the film finished.

In the film *Burden of Dreams,* documentary filmmaker Les Blank chronicles the chaotic production of Werner Herzog's epic film *Fitzcarraldo*. The documentary shows how Herzog's passion was the primary force that held together a production plagued with problems. The film had major casting problems, losing some lead actors for health or scheduling reasons, and halfway through production the crew became caught up in a war between Ecuador and Peru. Because the filming took four years, the cast and the crew became exhausted and demoralized. A less driven director would have given up on the project. Ironically, *Fitzcarraldo* itself was a film about a man passionately following his dream to bring opera to a jungle frontier town in South America. In the end, Herzog made his film, followed his dream, and shared the story he wanted so badly to tell.

Passion fuels action. Filmmakers consume the energy that their passion gives them in order to move forward and realize their films. Though the theme of the project may be universal, the

"My life? It's not very exciting. The excitement is the work. I live through my films. They are my life."
John Cassavettes

subject chosen can be unique. As with most project-based learning environments, I find that those that can encourage students to investigate subjects that fire their own passion will be fuelled with the most investigation and the most discovery. Consequently, these are the students who learn deeply and genuinely.

If we can help instill a passion for learning through these explorations, then we are helping to encourage important life-long learning characteristics that hopefully will seep through every part of their lives and whose benefits, though intangible, are priceless.

Empowerment

One of the opportunities in filmmaking is to empower students that what they do can make a difference. They learn that if there is something that they are not pleased with, something they don't agree with in their community, in their school, or in the world, they can take action to change it. That action can come in a form of a well-produced and concise piece of communication that we call film.

Perhaps the easiest way for students to believe this is possible is to provide examples from the real world. One of my favourite instances is from Alabama. Biology teacher John Sheffield[1] and his students have a living science lab known as the cliffs of Hurricane Creek situated close to their high school in Tuscaloosa, Alabama. For many years, Sheffield has brought students to study biology, geology, and entomology first hand, up close and personal.

Last year, the U.S. Department of Transportation announced an Interstate highway would be constructed and that the construction of a bypass would destroy the rare sandstone cliffs. The students and teacher went to the office of the Department of Transportation to see what could be done and were told to write letters, but that they should not hold out much hope for change. The local Sierra Club was also concerned about the destruction of the cliffs and,

"And it is hard to make a good movie. It's not just hard, it's nearly impossible —a feat that you bleed for and that you die for. And that's the way movies should be made. You may still say, 'I didn't communicate what I wanted to communicate,' or 'my movie's just not that great. I wish it was, but it's not.' But at least you die trying."
Jodie Foster

1
Classroom Video Magazine/Spring Summer 2001 / Pages 2-3.

together with Sheffield and his class, they embarked on a plan.

The students set about producing a video, explaining the importance of the cliffs, and their relevance to their learning, as well as some suggestions as to where the new bypass could be moved. The video was sent to the Department of Transportation, and to local interested people in the community. It made its way into the local newspaper and into the hands of the Governor of Alabama. The result? In time, the students received a letter from the Department of Transportation, which said:

"You will be pleased to know, based partly on the compelling presentation in the students' videos, I have instructed the design team developing the preliminary plans for the bypass project to shift the alignment as far to the east as possible within the design and environmental constraints. This will have the effect of minimizing impacts to the area of Hurricane Creek that is of concern to you and the students."

If students realize that they have the power, collectively or individually, to move a highway, what else will they realize that they have the power to change?

Team Building Skills

Filmmaking develops team building skills. As a director, my role is to work with members of my team and guide them to a shared goal. I do not work alone. A director must learn to communicate as both a listener and presenter of information. I must listen to concerns and ideas from actors, the crew and others, and through discussion and analysis, present scenarios that the entire team feels comfortable supporting and pursuing.

A filmmaking team may consist of a camera person, a sound recordist and a director, or it may be hundreds of artists and technicians. Regardless of the size of the team, a director must be able to keep them inspired and focused.

It is probable that when our students graduate they will be

working in environments where they will be members of some kind of a team. The filmmaking process in the classroom allows them to explore:

- What does it mean to be part of a team?
- How do you rely on others?
- How do others rely on you?
- What happens when someone in your team lets you down?
- How does it feel to let others down?
- How important is communication to a team?

There is much to be learned from the team approach. The challenges of finding consensus, listening to others, finding ways to compromise become additional learning experiences that will have real world relevance beyond the classroom.

Collaborative Skills

Sometimes filmmakers work on collaborative projects. This might be writers working together, a director working with a writer, an actor with a director, or any endless combination. What it is really about is two or more people with different creative perspectives coming together to create a new shared insight. It is a process that demands tolerance, understanding and a sense of adventure. Not all collaborations are successful, but certainly all are learning experiences for those involved.

Not only will students be working in teams in their future, but they will also have a need to collaborate with others in their professional and personal lives. They may be working with others in their communities as well as with others from around the world. They will experience different cultures, different point of views, and different sets of values.

The filmmaking process exposes students to the collaborative process and enables them to discover what ingredients contribute to successful partnerships and projects.

5: How Filmmaking Raises Awareness

Filmmaking fosters awareness. The investigative acts of research, preparation and planning bring in experiences to create new knowledge for the learner. The immersion in and familiarization with the subject creates a deep and lasting understanding. This understanding can begin an inquiry into the relationship between the subject and the filmmaker, and it is this awareness that can launch identification with community, peers, family and themselves.

Filmmaking allows us to explore new worlds. Filmmaking has the potential to spark meaningful connections when learners observe and explore subjects found outside their day-to-day environment. Creating this awareness allows students to investigate their own role and relationship to these new or different environments.

Sometimes it's about looking at the everyday in a new way. This can apply to investigation of our community or of our very own family. There are rich stories of human struggle and victories that remain untold simply because no one bothers to inquire.

I once made a film about my family. This film gave me permission to ask questions and to probe where everyday conversation would not normally lead or where decorum may prevent. At the end of this investigative journey of family and self, my own reward was a deeper awareness of what my parents and ancestors went through. Those stories were about what made us the family we are today, complete with all our success and failures, comic and tragic episodes, colourful characters, dashed hopes and miraculous interventions.

"The camera is a weapon against the tragedy of things, against their disappearing."
Wim Wenders

This is one of the greatest gifts that filmmaking offers…the ability to ask questions of our subjects for the benefit of our audience, and at the same time, for the benefit of ourselves.

The permission that filmmaking gave me to investigate my

family rewarded me with some insight into what it must have been like for my parents and grandparents to be immigrants in a new world. It has shaped how I see my own relationship and responsibility to my children, my family and my community.

Awareness of Family

One of my favourite examples of the potential of classroom video projects to create awareness to one's family is the splendid immigration project by Marco Torres. Marco is an Apple Distinguished Educator, Inspiration Educator of the Year, and video visionary. He teaches social studies in grades ten, eleven and twelve at San Fernando High School in California. Part of the learning outcomes that he guides his students towards falls under the topic of immigration. Torres and fellow teacher Mike Cady invited students to take a personal look at immigration. They invited students to create movies about their own family's personal history and immigration experience.

When I talked to Marcos, he shared some of the process with me. It is worth sharing, as it illustrates the process of the project, his process as an educator, and the nurturing learning environment of his classroom studio.

The project began with Marco inviting students to research their own families. They had to identify who their families were, when and where they were born, and when and how they came to California. They then looked at how they would tell their families' stories. Some looked at re-creating historical family events, others interviewed parents, grandparents and other relatives, and some used photographs and images. After deciding on a plan, they started filming and then editing.

After the assignments were completed, the students felt so good about their work that they insisted Marco show the films to their families. Parents and relatives were invited, the kids catered the event, the 'assignments' were presented to the families, and at

"I long for the day when I can be certain there's a filmmaker in every family, when the form of communication is not limited to the word or the page, when each kid can have a crack at giving a full expression to something of himself. How much richer the neighborhood would be, just one square block. We should be equipped and surrounded with the materials that creative activity calls for."
Nicholas Ray

the end of the evening there was not a dry eye in the room.

They investigated the topic of immigration through the personal perspective of their own family. In doing so, this project helped students raise awareness of their own family and create a connection to their own personal history.

Since family is something that both unites us and defines us, the inclusion of family in the project is a tremendous inspiration. Different families produce different histories. Different histories produce different videos. Like the student filmmakers themselves, they are all unique. What a great lesson to learn through a classroom project.

With so much discussion today about the erosion of families, perhaps this is another way in which filmmaking can help enrich students' lives beyond the exploration of content alone. Perhaps filmmaking may help in realizing that the families that we come from have specific human faces, names and stories. Perhaps learning that they were somehow important, courageous, adventurous, or even terrified, lonely, tenacious human beings can somehow help humanize the past and give our own lives a richer context.

Awareness of Social Issues

Many teachers are exploring the use of video production as a way for students to investigate the social issues that permeate their complex world. I have seen student videos that investigate bullying, peer pressure, AIDS, anorexia, steroids, information overload, smoking, drinking, dangerous driving, and other social issues.

Some are produced as documentaries, using interviews, text facts on screen, voice overs, stock videos and photos, and combinations of the above. Others are produced as dramas, with students acting out and having conversations related to these issues. Regardless of approach, here is a way to begin conversations about what really affects their lives.

This last year Linda and I worked with a grade twelve class at

Penticton Senior Secondary School, located in the southern part of the Okanagan Valley in British Columbia. The South Okanagan has the highest fatality rate of students dying from preventable driving accidents in all of British Columbia[4].

The video projects we assisted with were student-created Public Service Announcements and documentaries. The goal of this effort was to create videos that would have an impact upon their peers. The higher goal was to save young lives.

The filmmaking process led the students on an investigative journey into the world of driving accidents in and around our community. They interviewed police officers and heard stories of automobile accidents and the painful emptiness the officers felt approaching a house, knocking on a door and notifying parents that their child was killed in a car crash. They met with coroners and visited the morgue and the tables where the bodies of fellow students would have laid. They interviewed grief counsellors, insurance adjusters, tow truck drivers, paramedics, emergency room doctors and nurses and others who shared their clinical, often emotional, personal perspectives.

Through this investigation the students were able to appreciate a greater awareness of the impact that dangerous and deadly driving decisions make, not only for the person who is injured or killed, but also for the whole community.

Two weeks before filming was completed, a bright, popular, grade twelve girl died in a non-alcohol related driving accident. The realities of life and death became even more personal. What they hoped to do as filmmakers was to take the awareness they gained and share it with as many others as possible, and in doing so help prevent even one more unnecessary knock on someone's door.

[4] Interview by the author with Thomas Ingram, Insurance Corporation of British Columbia, May 2001, Penticton, British Columbia, Canada.

Awareness of Community

Students are interested and excited about working on

community-related projects because it gets them outside of the classroom. And I mean that both jokingly and seriously. Their bodies and minds are allowed to leave the schoolyard and join 'the real world.'

Communities are rich with opportunities for drawing connections between content and context. Learning outcomes come alive and have greater relevance by connecting community resources to student video projects. For example:

- The study of economics can become relevant when approached as a documentary of their favourite local business.
- Science outcomes can be imbedded in documentaries on local water treatment plants and the state of water quality in their area.
- Language Arts can come alive through interviews and stories.
- Social Studies can be examined through the eyes of citizens from diverse backgrounds.
- Mathematics can be uncovered in local architecture, computer programming, and in the home.
- Heritage, culture and artistic venues can provide rich information through the selection of thematic units.

There are as many opportunities for video projects in communities as there are different communities. In Part 2, we will begin the process of identifying and extracting these opportunities.

One of the many benefits of using your city or town as a backdrop for video exploration is that the construction of knowledge brings with it a construction of bridges. These are bridges between school and community, school and work, school and government and others. Partnerships can be formed, both formally and informally, and it is these partnerships that can bring flavours of the outside real world into the curriculum and to the student.

Real contact with the community creates empathy with the

subject. It is harder to vandalize a building when you have talked to the owner about his or her life and family. It is hard to dismiss someone because of race and background when you have shared a story or a smile.

Awareness of Self

Another opportunity inherent in filmmaking is the ability to develop a greater awareness of ourselves. Addressing subjects of a global, local or social nature inevitably leads us to question and examine our own perspectives and characteristics.

I recently worked with a group of grade six girls who were producing a twenty-minute film called *Friends*. It was a wonderful drama that they had written and performed. It looked at four friends and how the importance of fitting in with the cool students at school affected their relationship with each other.

The scriptwriting process itself was a series of questions. Would a character do this? Have I ever done something like this? Would I do this? Why would I? Do I know someone who has done this and how did I feel about that person? Filmmaking is asking questions.

As I worked with the girls during the evolution of the video, I would hear them ask each other personal questions, sometimes jokingly, sometimes seriously, debating, on behalf of their characters, the moral decisions that they were charged to make on and off the screen.

I believe that it is this opportunity to ask questions of ourselves, of relating external issues to personal circumstance, which makes the filmmaking process a powerful tool in helping us explore and identify who we are as human beings.

"The twisted circumstances under which we live is grist for the writing mill, the loving, hating and discovering, finding new handles for old pitchers…"
Alice Childress

Part 2:

The Filmmaking Process in the Classroom

"I think the funny thing about my movies is that, for all of my bilingual high schooling and Ivy League education, I make movies—intelligent movies—that are anti-intellectual. All of my intellectual processes have never brought me anything. They can help me describe things, but they're not experience. And experience is vastly, magically, totally and completely more interesting and more provocative.

But structure is very important, a language of that kind of left brain stuff is really important, and I think that's what's valuable about having come through such a traditional, structured, classic education."
Jodie Foster

The Filmmaking Process In the Classroom

In the first part of this book, we looked at why students should be making movies in the classroom. We looked at how filmmaking can integrate multiple educational objectives into fun project-based learning experiences and how the filmmaking process fosters real-life skills. In this next part, we will look at how each of the steps in the filmmaking process translates into rich learning opportunities. For this journey, we will follow two films: *Smoke* and *Water*. *Smoke* is based on a short drama that my wife Linda wrote, and *Water* is based on a classroom filmmaking project on water conservation.

Linda's scripts are a result of her fascination with people and her exploration of why people do the things they do. Specifically, in *Smoke,* she explores how people remember, especially when they know they are losing someone they love. Her passion for exploring the human condition fuels her writing. As filmmakers, it is our hope that this short film will connect to audiences and prompt their own investigation and awareness of themselves and the ones they love. This exploration is more about asking questions than providing answers.

The *Water* project is also a result of an exploration. It is fueled by students' passion to know about the world around them. The film is about why water conservation is important, what it means to their world and what can be done about it, but its end result is to stimulate discussion and action.

You will find the following forms discussed in this chapter in the Appendix and in PDF files on the enclosed CD :

Checklists:
- *Team Tasks*
- *Production*
- *Equipment*

Forms:
- *Project Criteria*
- *Contact List*
- *Location Survey*
- *Storyboard Template*
- *Scene Breakdown*
- *Shot List*
- *Shooting Schedule*
- *Budget*
- *Call Sheet*
- *Production Report*
- *Field Footage Log*
- *Work Timesheet*
- *Edit Decision List*

Release Forms:
- *Location*
- *Personal*
- *Copyright Materials*

The Five Phases of Filmmaking

A Brief Itinerary

If we were to go on an around-the-world adventure, we could pack our bags, step on a plane, see where it touches down, and begin exploring once we get there. However, we might prefer to know in advance where we are going, why we are going in that particular direction, and what we will see.

The filmmaking process is also an adventure. This part of the book will touch down on eleven ports of call spread over five different regions of filmmaking. So, before we begin the journey, here is a brief itinerary of where we are going.

The filmmaking process can be organized into five separate (though sometimes overlapping) phases. The five phases of the filmmaking process are:

1. Development
2. Pre-production
3. Production
4. Post-production
5. Distribution

1. Development (*Chapters 7–12*)

Before the actual filming of a movie can commence and before planning can begin, filmmakers must define the idea, the story and the project they are setting out to create. In filmmaking, the first phase is all about developing the project. The development phase includes:

- Writing (and rewriting) the script
- Determining what actors and what crew will be required
- Deciding who will direct the film
- Finding financing sources
- Investigating potential markets
- Developing preliminary schedules and budgets

"My movie is born first in my head, dies on paper; is resuscitated by the living persons and real objects I use, which are killed on film but, placed in a certain order and projected on to a screen, come to life again like flowers in water."
Robert Bresson

The following list outlines the major steps related to the development phase of classroom projects.

In the Classroom
- ❏ Define video project (scope, goals, time, genres)
- ❏ Determine student groups (groups determine roles)
- ❏ Hand out materials (time sheets, project sheets, etc.)
- ❏ Students work in their groups and develop ideas
- ❏ Students pitch project to instructor (and submit written materials)
- ❏ Instructor approves project (or asks for clarification or changes)
- ❏ Students write a script based on their presentation and submit for approval
- ❏ Instructor approves script (or asks for clarification or changes before approval)

2. Pre-production (*Chapters 12–13*)

Once a story becomes a script and there is an agreement as to what is to be filmed, pre-production can begin. The people required to execute the planning and production of the film are organized into 'departments,' and each of these departments begin analyzing exactly what is required to create the film. The Camera Department focuses on the camera requirements, the Sound Department on the sound requirements, and so on. There are detailed listings of the departments and their responsibilities in the next section.

The pre-production phase covers all the planning, research and preparation before the first day of shooting. This can be a few weeks, a few months, or sometimes a few years. On a professional film, it is often about three to six months.

In the Classroom
- ❏ Students prepare storyboards and submit for approval

❑ Instructor approves the storyboard
❑ Students prepare breakdown of requirements (locations, materials, people), shooting schedule and budget, and submit for approval
❑ Instructor approves planning documents
❑ Students make arrangements to use locations
❑ Students create props, costumes and sets

3. Production (*Chapter 14*)

At some point, the planning is complete and filming begins. The production phase begins with the first day of filming and ends when all the filming is completed. This phase is about recording images and sound that are required to tell a story or convey an idea. On a professional film the production phase often takes six to eight weeks, but may take fewer weeks or even a few years.

In the Classroom

❑ Students submit call sheets
❑ Students sign out and obtain equipment
❑ Students record video and audio
❑ Students return equipment
❑ Students submit production reports

4. Post-production (*Chapter 15*)

After filming is completed, it is time for editing to begin. Post-production involves everything that has to do with taking what was recorded and creating it into a finished film. This can sometimes mean the filming of additional footage, the purchasing of footage from 'stock libraries,' the re-recording of dialogue, the scoring of music, the creation of titles, the technical enhancement of each scene's colour and a screening to a test audience.

Post-production is complete once all the final decisions regarding the picture, audio, titles and graphics have been determined. It may be completed as a digital videocassette, a film print or even a digital file on a web site, but regardless, when it is ready to be seen by an audience, the film has finished post-production and begun distribution.

In the Classroom
- ❑ Footage is logged and captured
- ❑ Editing
  - • Picture editing
  - • Transitions
  - • Sound editing
  - • Titles and credits
- ❑ Test screening
- ❑ Revisions
- ❑ Project is exported to DV or VHS tape or exported as a digital movie file onto a CD, DVD or the Web.

5. Distribution (*Chapters 16–17*)

Distribution is about showing the film. It's about showing the film at festivals, on television, in video stores and anywhere else that audiences can be reached. It is about marketing the film, promoting the project and creating an awareness and excitement for potential audiences.

The distribution phase continues for many years, and for great films, it continues for decades.

In the Classroom
- ❑ Organize premiere (Don't forget the popcorn!)
- ❑ Students and instructors evaluate the project
- ❑ Films are submitted to festivals

7 The Filmmaking Team

Defining Student Roles

Have you ever watched the end credits of a movie and been amazed at how many people filmmaking involves? Filmmaking is a collaborative process, and it sometimes requires an 'army' of people to bring the magic on screen. Filmmaking's demand for many hands and many minds translates into opportunities for developing rich collaborative learning environments in the classroom.

The organization and communication that is required by students throughout the filmmaking process provides them with great opportunities to develop excellent planning and communication skills.

The number of students in a filmmaking team can vary greatly. Some projects are appropriate for individual students to create their own videos, much like they would produce their own report on a particular subject. In this case, students may draw upon assistance from other students, but the majority of the planning, filming and editing is executed by that one individual.

More ambitious projects may be designed as entire class projects, with students dividing up the responsibilities, and working together to create their film. Somewhere in-between these two is filmmaking teams of five or six students each. I like this size because it offers more hands-on learning experience than an entire class project, and more collaborative learning opportunities than solo projects.

There are no rules regarding the number and roles of students. These vary with the scope of the project, the resources of the school, the teacher's vision, and the ages and abilities of the students. What this implies, then, is a necessity for ongoing experimentation and adaptation.

Before we go on to explore the filmmaking process from idea to presentation, and how it translates into the classroom, I want to

"A poet needs a pen, a painter a brush, and a film-maker—an army," *Orson Welles.*

explore the roles and responsibilities of the filmmaking team and to briefly explain what the different crew members do.

Although you may never require this many categories on a student production, I include them here to help spark ideas on the potential of integrating all aspects of the creative process of filmmaking into the students' learning experience.

Departments

There are thousands of details to be considered in the journey of making a movie. Instead of filmmakers investigating all of these categories on their own, they often divide the responsibilities of planning and production into different departments.

A department can consist of a few, a dozen, or a hundred people, and is comprised of the artists and technicians who are involved with fulfilling that aspect of the filmmaking plan. Each department has a person in charge called a 'Department Head,' and the department heads lead their team through a series of logic-based examinations of what exactly is required to produce a film from the script provided.

Initially, the producer meets with all of the department heads individually, then collectively, to set out the vision for the project, and then on an ongoing basis to monitor their progress. The producer also works with each department head to identify and address the specific budget, scheduling and planning details specific to that department. Then the department heads lead their teams toward the common goals defined by themselves and the producer.

A list of some of the departments that filmmakers use in the planning and production of their films appears in the sidebar.

Departments in the Classroom: Defining Roles and Responsibilities

Depending on the kind of project, whether solo, team or entire

Accounting
Art Department
Assistant Director
Camera
Casting
Catering
Construction
Costume
Editing
Electrical
Grip
Hair
Lighting
Locations
Make Up
Props
Continuity
Production
Publicity
Set Decoration
Sound
Special FX
Stunt
Transportation

class, departments can be used as a way of dividing up the roles and responsibilities of filmmaking. They can also be used as a guide to systematically thinking through the requirements of the whole filmmaking process.

Individual Filmmakers

On projects where students are working individually, they will be responsible for all aspects of their own films.

The Individual Filmmaker's Checklist

Development
- ❑ Brainstorm and research ideas
- ❑ Pitch ideas and project
- ❑ Write Script

Pre-production
- ❑ Create Storyboard
- ❑ Create Scene Breakdowns
- ❑ Create Schedule and Budget

Production
- ❑ Create Shot List
- ❑ Obtain equipment
- ❑ Film required scenes
- ❑ Log footage
- ❑ Return equipment
- ❑ Create Production Report

Post-production
- ❑ Review footage
- ❑ Create paper edit
- ❑ Import footage into computer and edit picture, transitions, sound, titles and credits
- ❑ Export for viewing

Distribution
- ❑ Present finished film to class
- ❑ Organize additional screenings
- ❑ Produce publicity material

Teams of Five Filmmakers

Working as a team of five, students can take on the roles of writer, director, camera operator, editor and producer. Although each student will have a primary responsibility, each is expected to participate and assist with developing and researching the ideas as well as discussing and providing input into Storyboards, the pitch, the script, the planning, the production and the editing decisions.

With filmmaking teams of five, student roles and responsibilities may look something like the following chart throughout the five phases.

These, of course, are suggested divisions of responsibilities and should be experimented with constantly. Some students will complete their tasks prior to others during each phase of production. This is a great opportunity to remind them of their 'team role,' and suggest the re-direction of their resource (their time) towards the fulfillment of all the required tasks.

Large Group Projects

On more ambitious projects, the use of departments helps provide a framework for the involvement of individual students within large filmmaking teams.

Following are some suggested roles and responsibilities for working with large groups. Depending on the size of the groups and the ambitions of the project, these roles and responsibilities can be combined, deleted or modified. I must stress that departments are created not to divide the crew but to unite them. They are the essence of a strong team. The most successful filmmaking projects are a result of a cross-fertilization, not a compartmentalization, of energies and ideas.

Role descriptions and team tasks for a larger group follow the Team of 5 Filmmakers' Checklist.

Team of 5 Filmmakers' Checklist ■ ■ □

Development

Writer	❑ Writes Script
Director	❑ Leads brainstorming
Camera	❑ Researches visual imagery
Editor	❑ Leads research
Producer	❑ Pitches project

Pre-production

Writer	❑ Creates Scene Breakdown
Director	❑ Creates Storyboards
Camera	❑ Creates Shooting Schedule
Editor	❑ Creates Equipment and Contact Lists
Producer	❑ Creates Budget

Production

Writer	❑ Records sound
Director	❑ Determines what to shoot
Camera	❑ Operates the camera
Editor	❑ Logs field footage
Producer	❑ Creates Production Reports

Post-production

Writer	❑ Writes narration if required
Director	❑ Finds additional sounds and music
Camera	❑ Finds additional photos and video
Editor	❑ Operates editing system and determines final edit decisions
Producer	❑ Schedules editing equipment and assists team with editing and organizes test screenings

Distribution

Writer	❑ Writes Press Kit information
Director	❑ Organizes interviews
Camera	❑ Creates stills from videotape
Editor	❑ Produces promotional 'trailers'
Producer	❑ Organizes screenings

Executive Producer

...works with the producer(s) to ensure that a clear vision and plan for the project exists and that the filmmaking process advances smoothly. They listen to story ideas, review Storyboards, schedules, budgets and scene breakdowns. They supervise all aspects of filmmaking and have the right to ask questions and insist on clarification or revisions that put the project back on track. In classroom filmmaking projects, the teacher assumes the role of executive producer.

The Producer

...leads the filmmaking team through all phases of the film-making process. On a film set, they are the ones with their eyes glued to a watch and their ears glued to a phone. This cliché exists because of their constant attention to planning and scheduling.

The producer ensures that each department has the resources it requires in order to make its contribution to the overall project successful. The producer coordinates schedules, budgets and the flow of information. They are constantly checking with everyone to make sure things are on track and that obstacles are being overcome at every stage.

Production Manager

...assists the producer in ensuring that equipment and resources are available and scheduled for each department, and that the equipment has been returned. This person works closely with each department to coordinate department schedules and budgets.

Production Coordinator

...coordinates the flow of information between departments and assists the production manager and producer in their roles. The coordinator creates and maintains the cast and crew lists and also ensures that transportation is arranged to and from the location.

Producing Department • Team Tasks

Development
- ❑ Assists Executive Producer in organizing departments
- ❑ Helps develop project ideas
- ❑ Creates framework for brainstorming
- ❑ Works with writing department to ensure screenplay is completed
- ❑ Delivers screenplay to Executive Producer

Pre-production
- ❑ Creates and distributes Cast and Crew Contact List
- ❑ Collates department budgets, produces and distributes master Budget
- ❑ Collates department schedules, produces and distributes Shooting Schedule
- ❑ Ensures each department has the equipment and supplies they require
- ❑ Ensures that students acting in the film have signed permission slips

Production
- ❑ Ensures Call Sheets are produced and distributed
- ❑ Ensures transportation to location has been organized
- ❑ Ensures all production equipment and materials are present on the set
- ❑ Monitors production and assists in problem-solving
- ❑ Meets with Executive Producer and presents updates on schedules and budgets
- ❑ Produces and distributes Production Reports at end of each day's shooting

Post-production
- ❑ Ensures editing department has all audio and video materials required
- ❑ Ensures copyrighted material has been cleared (music, video, photos)
- ❑ Ensures all borrowed equipment has been returned
- ❑ Organizes test screenings and records audience feedback
- ❑ Delivers final film to Executive Producer

Distribution
- ❑ Ensures that screenings occur in school and elsewhere
- ❑ Ensures that film is submitted to film festivals
- ❑ Ensures that publicity department has necessary materials to promote the film

Director

…provides a cohesive vision of what the film will look like when it is finished and expresses that vision to the members of the filmmaking team. Thoroughly researches the project and the script and creates a vision of the finished work. The director articulates that vision through storyboards and shot lists.

He or she works with all the departments to ensure that each department's energies will contribute to achieving the desired product on the screen. Directors may be ultimately responsible for the creative execution of the film, but they do so through the input and collaboration of the entire filmmaking team.

Assistant Director

…assists the director with the preparation and production of the project. In Hollywood-style production, the assistant director works with the producers to ensure that the shot lists are ready, that shooting schedules are followed and that the obstacles to filming are removed. In the European definition, the assistant director is more like an apprentice who assists the director in articulating visual ideas (storyboards) and shooting plans. In the classroom, assistant directors would benefit by incorporating both styles.

The Director ■ ■ ■

Development

- ❑ Participates in brainstorming and developing ideas
- ❑ Researches content material related to the project
- ❑ Researches visual and audio ideas for the project
- ❑ Works with writing department to complete Script

Pre-production

- ❑ Supervises Storyboards
- ❑ Studies Script and becomes familiar with its goals, ideas and themes
- ❑ Meets with all departments to discuss production requirements
- ❑ Meets with producer to discuss schedules and budgets
- ❑ Rehearses actors

Production

- ❑ Prepares Shot Lists for each scene
- ❑ Works with camera department to set up each shot
- ❑ Ensures visual elements (sets, wardrobe, props, etc.) are as required
- ❑ Directs actors on set
- ❑ Determines when a shot has been performed competently
- ❑ Records the preferred shots for editing

Post-production

- ❑ Works with editing department to determine how to best tell the story with the audio and video materials available
- ❑ Works with editing department to find or produce additional material as required
- ❑ Attends test screenings and provides input for revisions
- ❑ Works with editing department to complete final version

Distribution

- ❑ Meets with media and provides interviews

The Writing Department

The writing department creates the screenplay document from which all planning and production flows.

Writers

…investigate and explore the subject of the film. They experiment with how to best tell the story in words and pictures and they write out their ideas in the form of a screenplay.

They research ideas, lead brainstorming sessions among themselves and others on the filmmaking team, and then synthesize the best ideas into a single, focused vision of what the story might be. Working with the director, they work towards telling the story as a series of scenes with strong visual elements and clear delivery of information.

In Hollywood-style productions, writers are not usually included in decisions having to do with pre-production (casting, locations, visual style), set improvisations or editing. In classroom filmmaking, however, I would recommend that their suggestions as storytellers could be valuable to the director and the production crew throughout the pre-production, production and post-production phases.

Writing Department • Team Tasks

Development
- ❑ Brainstorm and develop ideas
- ❑ Research content material related to the project
- ❑ Research visual and audio ideas for the project
- ❑ Work with Director and Producer to complete the Script

Pre-production
- ❑ Continue rewriting the Script as required
- ❑ Assist director in creating Storyboard

Production
- ❑ Assist Director in preparing Shot Lists for each scene
- ❑ Consult with Director as to which shots may be best for editing, and record that information
- ❑ Assist in improvising dialogue or rewriting scenes on location

Post-production
- ❑ Work with editing department to determine how to best tell the story with the audio and video materials available
- ❑ Works with editing department to find or produce additional material as required
- ❑ Write narration if required
- ❑ Attend test screenings and provide input for revisions

Distribution
- ❑ Write Press Kit information

The Locations Department

The location department exists to research, suggest and manage locations for the filming of the scenes of the script.

Location Scout

…researches where the filming will take place. They read the script, consult with the other members of the filmmaking team, and then set off to uncover possible locations.

They record what locations they visit with photographs or with video and then make a presentation to the team. This presentation includes recommendations by the scout of what locations they recommend and why. In addition to taking photographs and video, they document the location's address, contact person and other information that the production team may require.

Location Manager

Once a location has been selected, the location scout or the location manager will meet with the location contact person and detail in writing when the crew will arrive, where exactly they will be recording, how long they will be staying, and what is required, if anything, of the contact person.

The location manager is responsible for organizing logistics such as parking, washroom access, general access, and food considerations, as well as being a liaison with the location contact throughout the filming process.

Locations Department • Team Tasks ■ ■ □

Development

- ❑ Research other videos, films and works of art for ideas on the use of location to enhance the film's ideas, goals and themes

Pre-production

- ❑ Create location breakdowns to determine what sets are required
- ❑ List possible locations for each set
- ❑ Scout possible locations and complete location survey for each location
- ❑ Photograph or videotape each location
- ❑ Present locations to team with recommendations
- ❑ Secure locations
- ❑ Create department Schedule and Budget

Production

- ❑ Create schedule of locations and when they will be required
- ❑ Communicate with location contact to inform and schedule arrival
- ❑ Coordinate arrival and departure

Post-production

- ❑ Ensure that location was left clean and orderly
- ❑ Send thank you cards to the location contact

Distribution

- ❑ Invite location contact person to a screening

The Art Department

The art department creates the visual ingredients of a film. The art department identifies exactly how the visual look of the film will come together and articulates who will be responsible for creating or providing the sets, props, set dressings, make-up, hairstyles and wardrobe that will be required.

Production Designer

...responsible for coordinating the efforts of all the members of the art department and for providing visual ideas and suggestions to the production.

Set Designer

...designs the sets and backdrops to be used in the production.

Set Dresser

...determines what items will be used to dress the set. For example, on a kitchen set, it may be tables and chairs, a refrigerator, paintings on the wall, curtains on the window, or a row of spice jars on a counter.

Property Master

...determines what items the actors will handle. For example, on a kitchen set, the actors may handle a bread knife, a piece of toast, a newspaper, a pair of eyeglasses, a jar of honey, a wallet or a cup of hot coffee.

Costume/ Hair/ Make-up Supervisors

Sometimes on smaller films, one person will be responsible for all the costume, hair and make-up requirements. If a specific project, a historical re-enactment or example, requires more attention to costumes, hair and make-up, then one student would be responsible for each of these categories.

Art Department • Team Tasks   ■ ■ ■

Development
- ❑ Brainstorm visual ideas
- ❑ Research visual ideas
- ❑ Provide visual aids for pitching ideas and project

Pre-production
- ❑ Create breakdowns of visual requirements
- ❑ Create art department Schedule and Budget
- ❑ Design, create or source sets, costumes, props, dressing, hair and make-up

Production
- ❑ Assemble sets and provide set dressings and props
- ❑ Costume actors and provide hair and make-up where necessary
- ❑ Source last-minute ideas

Post-production
- ❑ Return borrowed items with thank you cards
- ❑ Store created materials in classroom studio

Distribution
- ❑ Create visual materials for Press Kit
- ❑ Create posters for screenings

The Camera Department

The camera department is responsible for recording the scenes and images that describe the ideas and stories of the film.

Director of Photography (D.O.P)

…helps the director determine what images will be recorded and how they might be recorded. Together they discuss camera angles, lighting ideas, camera movement, lens choices and any other details surrounding the recording of the image. The D.O.P. works with the lighting department to design the lighting for each shot and works with the grip department to design how the camera will be placed (stationary or moving).

Camera Operator

…operates the video camera during the production. They look at the scene through the viewfinder or the screen and adjust the composition and movement of the lens to follow the action that takes place.

Camera Assistant

…assists the camera operator with the handling of the camera and ensures that batteries, extra tapes, and AC power supply are available as required. Marks scenes with slate to identify what scene and what take is being recorded.

Development

Camera Department • Team Tasks ■ ■ ❑

Development

❑ Research visual imagery from works of art and other videos and movies

Pre-production

❑ Determine what camera equipment is required and sources that equipment

❑ Test camera equipment prior to filming and familiarize themselves with all aspects of the camera package

❑ Discuss lighting ideas with lighting department

❑ Discuss camera movement ideas with grip department

❑ Create department Schedule and Budget

Production

❑ Bring all required camera equipment to set

❑ Set up camera, sets white balance for the lighting being used, test records

❑ Mark slate to identify which take and which scene is being recorded

❑ Move camera smoothly during pans and tilts, ensure focus

❑ Ensure there is enough video tape in camera before each take

❑ Indicate to the sound department when the boom microphone is in frame

❑ Advise director if video recording is out of focus, or not properly executed and suggest methods to improve the recording on the next take

❑ Create Field Footage Reports that clearly identify what was shot

❑ At end of day, carefully store and return camera package

Post-production

❑ Liaise with editors to identify all recorded footage

❑ Re-shoot missing scenes or images if required

❑ Research additional video material (stock video footage)

❑ Send thank you cards for borrowed equipment

Distribution

❑ Videotape interviews for electronic Press Kit

The Sound Department

The sound department ensures that voices and sounds are recorded as clearly as possible in order to help articulate the ideas and stories of the video.

Production Sound Mixer

...supervises the placement of microphones on the set and determines when to use booms, tie clip microphones and hidden microphones. The sound mixer also suggests and supervises ways to diminish distracting sounds from outside the set and monitors the sound recording at all times.

Boom Person

...places the boom (a long pole with the microphone attached) as close to the actors as possible in order to obtain the clearest recording. The boom person also helps the production mixer with the placement of additional microphones as required, and ensures there are no boom shadows in the shot and that the boom does not dip into the frame.

Cable Person

...assists the boom person with the handling of the microphone cables as well as assists the production mixer and boom person with any other requirements related to audio recording.

Sound Department • Team Tasks ▪ ▪ ▪

Development

❏ Develop and research ideas related to sound design from other videos, movies and audio works

Pre-production

❏ Determine what kind of sound recording will be required
❏ Determine what kinds of microphones will be required
❏ Source microphones
❏ Assess location's suitability in terms of existing noise and traffic
❏ Create department Schedule and Budget

Production

❏ Arrange and pick up audio equipment
❏ Link the external microphones to the camera
❏ Establish the best location of microphones for each shot
❏ Use boom poles to place microphones close to actors
❏ Monitor dialogue through headsets
❏ Advise Director if audio recording is unclear and suggest methods to improve the audio recording on the next take
❏ Record ambient sound on each set (room tone)
❏ Provide audio reports, detailing what audio was recorded

Post-production

❏ Record additional sounds as required
❏ Re-record dialogue if required
❏ Record musicians and bands for music score if required
❏ Work with sound editor to ensure efficient locating of audio recording

Distribution

❏ Record interviews for publicity materials

The Lighting and Grip Department

The lighting department creates the light and shadows of the images on screen. The grip department assists the lighting department and is also responsible for providing and operating equipment used to move the camera during each scene. On smaller films, the roles overlap or combine.

Gaffer

…discusses lighting ideas with the director and director of photography and organizes the equipment and people to execute the lighting plan. The lighting plan dictates which lights will be used, where the lights will be set up, in which direction they will be pointed and how they might be filtered or diffused. The gaffer also considers any other details that will affect the illumination of the objects on screen.

Best Boy

…assists the gaffer with the selection and placement of lights. Ensures the safety of the equipment on the set with properly secured lighting stands and properly laid lighting cables.

Key Grip

…arranges the setting up of light stands and reflectors, assists with the movement of equipment for all departments, secures the camera wherever it is placed, and assists personnel in other departments.

Dolly Grip

…understands how the director and director of photography wish the camera to move and arranges and operates the equipment for it to do so. The piece of equipment most often used to move the camera during a shot is called a dolly, hence the name.

Dolly & Grip Department • Team Tasks ■ ■ ▫

Development
- ❑ Research ideas related to lighting from other videos, movies and works of art

Pre-production
- ❑ Assess locations for lighting obstacles and opportunities
- ❑ Assess locations for camera movement obstacles and opportunities
- ❑ Determine what kind of lighting and grip equipment will be required
- ❑ Source or create lighting and grip Equipment List
- ❑ Consult with the Director and Director of Photography regarding lighting ideas
- ❑ Consult Storyboards for lighting objectives
- ❑ Consult Storyboards for camera movement objectives
- ❑ Create department Schedule and Budget

Production
- ❑ Safely set up light stands and lights
- ❑ Safely lay extension cords and cables from lights to power outlets
- ❑ Arrange lights as per lighting plan
- ❑ Monitor the effect of light on the set
- ❑ Consult with director of photography to fine-tune lighting effects
- ❑ Move camera smoothly (using wheelchairs, tracks, swivel chairs, etc.)
- ❑ Allow lights to cool, then disassemble them for storage and handling

Post-production
- ❑ Provide grip and lighting for any additional videotaping

Distribution
- ❑ Provide grip and lighting for videotaping any press-related interviews

The Editing Department

The editing department assembles all the audio and video material that has been created and collected and transforms it into a single finished video.

Post-production Supervisor

…supervises the flow of audio and video materials from the production crew to the editing team. Works with the producer to book equipment and determine editing schedules.

Editor

…selects which audio and video segments best tell the story and includes those in the assembly edit. The editor experiments with different takes, different camera angles, transitions, titles and visual enhancements such as colouring or filtering.

Sound Editor

…concentrates on the music, the sound effects, the atmospheric sound and the dialogue that are included in the soundtrack. The sound editor focuses on enhancing each piece of sound that is used for each scene.

Assistant Editor

…assists the editors by importing and logging footage into the editing system and keeping track of videotapes and other materials.

Development

Editing Department • Team Tasks

Development
- ❑ Research ideas related to editing styles

Pre-production
- ❑ Consult Storyboards and become familiar with the editing intent of the production
- ❑ Make a list of audio, video and photographic materials required for editing separate from what is being recorded (for example: stock footage, music, sound effects)
- ❑ Create department Schedule and Budget

Production
- ❑ Find or produce the additional materials required for editing
- ❑ Work with sound department to record additional sounds required for editing
- ❑ Work with camera department to record additional video where required

Post-production
- ❑ Ensure footage logs exist of all materials
- ❑ Create paper edit
- ❑ Import camera footage into editing system
- ❑ Assemble rough cut
- ❑ Create picture cut with visual transitions and titles
- ❑ Add soundtracks containing music, sound effects or narration
- ❑ Export project for test screening
- ❑ Produce final edited version
- ❑ Export project for distribution

Distribution
- ❑ Work with unit publicist to create Electronic Press Kit

The Publicity Department

The publicity department creates and collects promotional materials such as photographs, videotape, interviews and text materials that document the process of creating the film. The material is then used at the completion of the project to help promote awareness of the film to audiences.

Unit Publicist

…plans and coordinates the collection of the marketing and promotional materials. The unit publicist works with the producer to coordinate times for interviews and media visits. They also coordinate the distribution of promotional materials to media and festivals.

Unit Photographer

…works with the unit publicist and producer to determine the kinds of promotional photographs required and is responsible for their acquisition. The unit photographer records both candid shots of people at work, as well as staged portraits of cast and crew.

Unit Videographer

…works with the unit publicist and producer to determine the kind of video clips required and is responsible for their acquisition. The unit videographer records both candid shots of people at work, as well as staged interviews of cast and crew.

Publicity Department • Team Tasks ■ ■ ■

Development
- ❑ Research ideas related to publicizing the final video

Pre-production
- ❑ Design Press Kit and determine what materials should be collected during production
- ❑ Photograph and videotape 'behind the scenes' of the different departments at work
- ❑ Plan when and how publicity interviews will occur
- ❑ Create department Schedule and Budget

Production
- ❑ Photograph and videotape the crew at work on the set
- ❑ Photograph and videotape 'behind the scenes' work of the departments
- ❑ Conduct interviews with all personnel
- ❑ Contact local newspapers and media (if desired) to photograph and interview student filmmakers

Post-production
- ❑ Conduct additional interviews
- ❑ Photograph and videotape editing department at work
- ❑ Pull together visual and text elements for press kits

Distribution
- ❑ Coordinate local media to attend screenings (if desired)
- ❑ Arrange interviews between student filmmakers and media
- ❑ Organize and ship Press Kits
- ❑ Provide press material for submission to film festivals

8: Designing Great Filmmaking Projects

What makes a great filmmaking project?

This part of the book is about creating great filmmaking projects, but what exactly makes a project great? I believe that great projects should:

- Be relevant to the students' world
- Provide opportunities for creating awareness of community, family and self
- Provide opportunities for developing higher order thinking skills
- Provide opportunities to experience real world learning
- Above all, be enjoyable experiences

The best way to explore what makes a project great is to dissect the ingredients of its design. In this chapter, we will ask, "What questions can be applied, at each step, that could help elevate the project into a memorable and meaningful learning experience for all involved?"

How to Begin

Our first step in filmmaking is to define exactly what it is we want to do. Before research begins, before cameras are unpacked and long before actors and crew perform their magic, the filmmaker begins the journey by asking questions:

- What do we want to investigate?
- What interests us?
- What do we care about?
- What are we really passionate about?
- What matters to my world, to my family and to me?
- …and the most complex of simple questions: What is our purpose?

For some, the purpose of making films is to entertain. For others it is to inform. Others make films to convince, argue or defend points of view. Ultimately, most filmmakers make films to

"It's not a question of my own satisfaction or lack of it, but of the basic purpose of a film, which I believe is one of illumination, of showing the viewer something he can't see any other way. And I think at times this can be best accomplished by staying away from his own immediate environment. This is particularly true when you're dealing in a primarily visual experience, and telling a story through the eyes. You don't find reality only in your own backyard, you know—in fact, sometimes that's the last place you find it."
Stanley Kubrick

"I like to act in films, I like to shoot 'em, I like to direct 'em, I like to be around 'em. I like the feel of it and it's something I respect. It doesn't make any difference whether it's a crappy film or a good film. Anyone who can make a film, I already love. But I feel sorry if they don't put any thought in it because then they missed the boat."
John Cassavettes

explore. They explore what they are most passionate about.

The film may be about exploring cultural, political or social topics through documentaries (like the student film, *Water*). It may be about exploring human actions through dramas (like our short drama, *Smoke*). Whether drama or documentary, the ideas and issues that we are interested or passionate about need to be translated from intangible themes into specific subjects. We cannot film the act and circumstances of memory, nor can we film the concept of ecology, but we can explore each through the specific.

Memory is examined through the exploration of four people with differing perspectives on life and death. Ecology is examined though the exploration of water conservation in our community. Each uses a visible tangible subject to explore a greater idea.

So we begin with the question, "What is the purpose?"

As a way to keep track of notes and to work through the project design, I often use a tool I call a Guide to Designing Great Projects.

Guide to Designing Great Projects ■ ■ ■	
Purpose:	
Vision:	
Subject:	
Questions:	
Production Team:	
Format:	
Project Length:	
Delivery Date:	
Audience:	
Venue:	
Delivery Format:	
Special Instructions:	
Assessment:	

Purpose

The first question on the sheet is: What is the purpose? We decide that the purpose for the *Water* project is to raise awareness and foster students' exploration of ecological issues and how they relate to the world they live in. And so we begin.

Purpose:	To raise awareness and foster exploration of ecological issues and how they relate to the world they live in.

Vision

Now before we go further, indulge me for a moment. Let me be so bold as to suggest that the next step is to dream. The challenge is to dream, and to dream big. In your wildest dreams, what would you love to see this finished project achieve? Thinking far into the future, what would you love to have your students experience? For this project, I have something in mind.

Vision:	To lead initiatives which improve water conservation in our community.

This vision may sound ambitious, but the point is that I want filmmaking projects to be about something and ideally, something that matters to students and to their world. I try to dream up projects that help students realize that they have the potential to improve the world that they live in. This may be ecological, as in the *Water* project. It may be social, economic or cultural. It aims to change something in their community or at least open up conversation and create awareness. If a classroom project initiates dialogue and debate, and invites action, students will get it. They will realize their potential to be agents of change. That would be a great success for everyone.

"I never film what I don't want. I am not interested in making films where I am forced to raise money. Whether it's good or not, one must be strong. The film maker must believe in something, be honest with himself, and be objective in his job."
Akira Kurosawa

One of the schools I am working with is located near a desert. The Desert Centre, <*www.desert.org*> in Osoyoos, British Columbia is an ecological interpretive centre that exists to provide information to schools and to the public on the plant, animal, and geographical characteristics of the Osoyoos desert as well as desert ecology, ecological restoration and endangered ecosystems conservation. The filmmaking assignment that the grade seven students will be producing will follow an ecological theme and will explore regional ecosystems, the impact of civilization on the environment and strategies for sustaining their unique piece of geography. But that's not what I tell them.

I walk into the class and I say, "Who wants to help me save a desert? I tell them about the plants, animals and geographic characteristics of their nearby desert and how it is being destroyed.

I explain that we are going to make some movies about the desert, and about what goes on there and what is happening to it. And when the movies are finished, that they will be put on the web site of the Desert Centre. People from around the country and around the world will learn more about this specific part of our planet through the movies that they, the students, will produce. I want to make it clear to them that this project is not only about handing in an assignment in order to receive a grade, it is about being active participants who can help shape their planet's destiny. My goal is to transplant a passion for the project at that high a level.

Some might say, "But not everything we teach is about making the world a better place," and my response is, "Then why not?" What is the relevance and why should it matter to kids? If we can't demonstrate passion about what science, social studies, English, math or drama has to do with the world that students live in, how can we expect them to care? How can we expect them to be inspired learners? Of course this is a great challenge, but I believe it is of the utmost importance.

Subject

Let's go back to the *Water* project. What will the film be about? Since we cannot film ecology itself, we need to define the specific subject that relates to ecology. The teacher might define this, but it might also be discovered by the class. What if water conservation were first talked about in class and then the question posed, "How can we help our community conserve water?" Suggestions might be, "By putting posters around town," or "By writing articles for the local newspapers." But ask the class, "What about by making a movie? Would you like to make a movie that will save our planet? Yes? Then what should the movie be about exactly? What questions should it answer? Let's write down what the movie is about and call that our subject."

Subject: Water conservation in our community

Questions

To be more specific, and to continue the shaping of this project, let's ask, "What questions will this movie answer?"

Think of movies as answers to questions. Dramatic movies and feature films sometimes answer questions like, "What if you could see the impact your life has had on others?" One answer to that question is the movie *It's a Wonderful Life* [1] with Jimmy Stewart. Or in a documentary it may be "What happens when people are so poor they are forced to try and change the world in order to survive?" and the answer may be *A Place Called Chiapas: Eight Months Inside the Zapatista Revolution*.[2]

"All my life I've fought against clarity—all those stupid definitive answers. Phooey on a formula life, on slick solutions. It's never easy. I think it's only in the movies that it's easy. I won't call (my work) entertainment. It's exploring. It's asking questions of people. A good movie will ask you questions you haven't been asked before."
John Cassavettes

1. *It's a Wonderful Life*, directed by Frank Capra in 1946 is the story of an angel who helps a man in despair by showing him the profoundly positive impact that the man has had on his community.

2. On January 1, 1994, the Zapatista National Liberation Army, made up of impoverished Mayan Indians from the state of Chiapas, took over five towns and 500 ranches in southern Mexico. The Government deployed its troops, and at least 145 people died in the ensuing battle. Fighting for indigenous Mexicans to regain control over their lives, and the land, the Zapatista Army, led by the charismatic, guerilla poet Subcommandante Marcos, started sending their message to the world via the Internet. The result was what The New York Times called "the world's first post-modern revolution." Filmmaker Nettie Wild traveled to the jungle canyons of southern Mexico to film the elusive and fragile life of the uprising. Her camera (Nettie Wild and Kirk Tougas) effectively and movingly captures the human dimensions behind this war of symbols.

In our classroom, the question may be, "Why is it important to conserve water in our community?" and the answer is the film that is produced. There will be more questions that will become part of the project, like what is water conservation, what are people doing right, what are people doing wrong, and what should be done, to name a few, but at this point, let's keep focused on the exploration of "Why is water conservation important?"

> Question: **Why is water conservation important?**

As educators, we have a choice of crafting a project ourselves or involving the class in the decision-making process. The benefit of the class involvement is of course the students' ownership of the filmmaking project and ultimately, ownership of their own learning experience.

So far, we have defined that we will be producing films that ask and answer questions about water conservation. Now we get more specific.

Production Teams

Filmmaking is a collaborative process that brings together the talent and energy of many artists from a variety of professions and backgrounds. Feature films often have hundreds of personnel involved through the various stages of the filmmaking process, but they also have been made with fewer than a dozen. Documentaries are often made by dozens of crew but have also been made by a single filmmaker doing everything themselves. There is no law or set standard of how many people are required are on the film crew. The number usually comes from the simple question, "How many people can we afford?"

For the student film, *Water*, we must decide how many people will be in the production team. Production teams can be the entire class or a single student. Short projects may be individual efforts while dramatic or adventurous documentaries may take the combined talent and energy of the entire class. Most common, though, is to create groups of four to six students to allow for maximum hands-on experience and to facilitate communication.

Let's say that groups of five will allow collaborative skills to be developed and responsibilities delegated between producer, director, writer, camera person and editor.

> Production Team: **5 per Team, Producer, Director, Camera, Writer, Editor**

Format

The next step for our *Water* project is to define what form the film will take. Filmmaking has many forms. There are documentary films, experimental films, animated films (cell, paper, electronic, clay), and narrative films (comedies, dramas, action, etc.), and there are also hybrids of all of the above. Educators have been using film and video in the classroom for many years, for a variety of projects whose formats include:

- Documentaries
- Narrative Dramas
- Experimental
- Dance
- Animation
- Commercials
- Public Service Announcements
- News-style reporting
- Talk Show format
- Game shows

"The length of a film should be directly related to the endurance of the human bladder."
Alfred Hitchcock

The exploration of *Water* could probably be achieved in any of the above forms, even including the game show. It could be done as a public service announcement, or a drama. I once saw a play that was set in the future and was about a war that was being raged for the ownership of clean water because it had become more precious than oil or gold.

The different filmmaking groups could investigate and evaluate different formats for the *Water* project and decide which format they wish to use. For now, let's say that we go with a documentary approach. This may include the use of interviews, historic photographs, archival film footage, maps, charts, narration and more.

> Format: **Documentary**

Duration

What is the duration of our *Water* project? Films come in many shapes and sizes. There are feature length films that run for an hour and a half or more, and there are short films that are less than a minute. Everything is possible, but the question is, "Which is the most appropriate?"

If you are producing a commercial or a public service announcement, then a 30 or 60-second finished duration is appropriate to that film form. Documentaries can range from minutes to hours, but in a classroom setting, under ten minutes seem to be a favourite duration while feature length projects are rare because of the time required.

Having said that, I invite you to prove me wrong and send me your feature length projects! Dramas can be more time consuming than documentaries because of the more complex coordination of creating a reality instead of filming one. Five-minute dramas can take weeks or months to prepare for, depending on how much class time is available. It will change with every teacher, every group of students, and every age level.

Let's say that we set the duration for each film to be five minutes, including head (beginning) and ending titles.

> Duration: 5 minutes including titles

Delivery Date

In the real world of filmmaking, it's all about schedules, and about how much time there is to make the film. Is it a year, a month, a day? Filmmaking requires preparation, production and editing; all of these take time. At some point, the distributor of the film will require that the film be delivered to them. The date that the distributor requires the completed project 'handed in' is referred to as the 'delivery date.' I like to use this term with students because it is fun to use real world language, specifically motion picture terms, and in doing so, provide another connection to life outside their school.

Let's look at *Water*. Is this project going to be a one-day activity, a one-week activity, a one-month activity, or an activity that will take place over the entire school year? As we will see later on, the pressure of not enough time (which is almost always the case when you are making a movie) is actually a great opportunity for developing problem solving skills that include learning about scheduling, budgeting and resource management.

Let's give ourselves a month to make these movies.

> Delivery Date: One month from today

Audience

The purpose of making a film comes from the goal of the filmmaker to communicate an idea to others. Filmmakers do not realize their goal until it has been brought to an audience and their ideas have been shared. Filmmakers may have a specific audience in mind or their audience may be broad. The film may be for a specific age or understanding, or it may be for a specific cultural, social or economic interest group.

Students like to see their work presented to an audience and if that audience is limited to their teacher, we rob them of a greater experience. When students know that their audience is the rest of the school, or the community, or the world, they tend to sit up and take the project a little more seriously.

Who is the audience for *Water*? Let's suggest, as a start, that it will be the people who live in the students' community. It may be audiences of all ages and all interests, since the existence of clean water is, or should be, a concern for all. So in this case, we will leave the audience as broad.

Audience: Everyone in the community

Venue

Filmmakers reach audiences through cinemas, film festivals, television, videos and in today's digital world, through CD, DVD and the World Wide Web.

How can audiences see student movies? In the same way. Student projects have been seen on television, at student and other film festivals, on CDs, DVDs and on the World Wide Web. In addition, the school assembly can be a venue for student work or a special evening of student work can be screened with the community invited to attend. Local community cable companies can broadcast student projects on their networks. Local video rental stores can have complimentary copies to lend out. There are numerous ways to reach audiences.

For the project *Water*, what other venues might be considered, in addition to those already mentioned? Can we show these finished films to the city council, perhaps at a special presentation? Can they be played at City Hall as people line up to pay their water bills? Can they play at hardware stores that sell water conservation supplies? Can they be placed on the community's web site?

The possibilities are only limited by the imagination of the teacher and the filmmaking groups. I am sure that you, reading this, can come up with even more ideas!

Let's say our goal is to have a premiere in one of the meeting rooms at City Hall, invite the community down to watch, and have the city support an awareness campaign on water conservation. A bit ambitious dream? Sure, but that's part of the fun, to stretch our reach and potential. It can be done.

Venue: City Hall meeting room

Delivery Materials

The delivery materials lists exactly what is expected from the filmmaker on the delivery date. On a Hollywood-style project it may state the format the finished film is to be delivered in (35mm film, Digital Betacam, DV Cam, High Definition Video, etc.). Filmmakers sometimes have to submit materials in addition to the finished film. These materials may include a copy of the script, a cast and crew list, a list of music and other copyrighted materials that are on the program, and publicity materials.

For classroom projects like *Water*, identifying the format of the finished film is necessary in order to be able to play the film for the audience at the specified location. In practical terms, it's an opportunity to explicitly state what is required for the student to deliver in order to complete the assignment.

For our city hall premiere, we will be best off if the tapes are finished on Mini DV and then all the tapes can be edited together onto one Mini DV tape. Remember Digital Video tape does not degrade with each dub as do analog formats like VHS or Hi8. Plus, if we have access to a DVD burner, we could produce a DVD, which we could then play from a home DVD machine. But let's stick with the Mini DV tape.

> Delivery Material: **Mini DV Tape**

Special Instructions

Sometimes filmmakers have to create their original works while working with some special instructions from the film's producer, studio or distributor. For example, they may have to include a particular star to play a character. Or they may have to shoot at a particular location. Or they may have to shoot in a specific film format. (Films that are destined for theatres and television, for example, often must be filmed so that the framing looks best for television, not for theatres.)

On this part of the project sheet teachers can put their own list of special instructions; for example, for the *Water* project, the special instructions may include:

> Special Instructions:
> - Use at least one interview
> - Use both interior and exterior locations
> - Identify 5 examples of poor water management
> - Present 3 recommendations for water conservation

Assessment

Filmmakers release their films to theatres and are assessed by the movie-going public and the movie critics. Positive reviews and audience approval provide filmmakers with financial and emotional rewards. Negative reviews suggest that they have failed to connect with their audience or clearly express their ideas. I say this in a general way, as there have been great films that have been overlooked by critics for many years only to be 'understood' years later. But for our purposes let's say that filmmakers undergo some type of assessment.

The final step in designing a great project is to consider assessment strategies and then, ideally, to have the students themselves included in the design of their own assessment.

There are many possibilities for meeting cross-curriculum objectives in a filmmaking project. A teacher that I interviewed put it this way, "Yes, filmmaking projects take a little more energy to organize, but you can cover so many subjects with one single project that you actually can save a lot of classroom time with a little good planning."

The *Water* project, for example, contains learning outcomes associated with:

• Ecology and Life Science (the subject of this film)

But also with:

• Self and Society (Personal Awareness)
• Self and Society (Working Together)
• Self and Society (Building Community)
• The Planning Process (Scheduling, Planning)
• Mathematics (Budgets, Estimating)
• Language Arts
  - Communicating Ideas and Information
  - Presenting and Valuing
  - Improving Communications
  - Composing and Creating
  - Comprehending and Responding

      - Strategies and Skills
      - Comprehension
      - Engagement and Personal Response
      - Critical Analysis

Filmmaking projects can, and should, incorporate multiple learning objectives, and time spent investigating these crossover areas will serve to make the project ripe for assessment possibilities.

Assessment: **Assessment Rubric**

Assessment Rubric

Movie critics exist to critique movies. They watch a film and then present the public with their evaluation of the film's success in communicating ideas. The famous two thumbs up sign of approval from film critics Roger Ebert and Gene Siskel has now become part of our culture.

Movies are art, and art is subjective, so no two people are going to see a movie in the same way. As audiences, we bring to the viewing our own histories and unique points of view. In an attempt to critique objectively, movie critics evaluate the film based on the different components that created it. They may comment that the cinematography was outstanding, the music haunting, the performances inspired, the sets outlandish, the editing gripping, or the main idea powerful and well communicated. They may also add their personal points of view, interpretations and feelings about why that film did or did not work.

Educators have the opportunity to treat the assessment of student filmmaking projects as if they were film critics reviewing a movie. Definable components of the student films can be objectively assessed to produce less subjective critiques.

As an educator, you might begin by asking your students: What makes a great film? What makes a not so great film, and how do we tell the difference? How can we objectively grade films?

What are the components that film critics use and what can we use, as a class, to assess our own films?

Here are a very few suggestions:
- **Technical:**   Camera work
                     Sound
                     Lighting
                     Editing
- **Creative:**   Was the project question answered?
                     Were examples used to back up ideas?
                     Were original ideas presented?
                     Were words spelled correctly?

Then, looking at each of these questions (and many more), you might ask your students what specific characteristics can be distinguished between unsatisfactory, satisfactory, great and outstanding work for each component?

One suggestion is to use a rubric to match each potential category of assessment with each characteristic of proficiency. For example, the sound component alone could be subdivided into the categories of overall sound quality, use of music, use of narration and use of sound effects. (This is an abbreviated version, with a more detailed chart in chapter nineteen.)

	Unsatisfactory (1)	Satisfactory (2)	Great (3)	Outstanding (4)
Technical				
1) Sound a) Overall	Audio track cannot be understood most of the time.	Audio track is difficult to hear.	Audio can be heard clearly, but has occasional extraneous noises and pops.	Audio track is error free.

Guide to Designing Great Projects ■ ■ ■

Purpose:	To raise awareness and foster exploration of ecological issues and how they relate to the world we live in
Vision:	To lead initiatives that improve water conservation in our community
Subject:	Water conservation in our community
Questions:	Why is water conservation important?
Production Team:	5 per team: Producer, Director, Camera person, Writer, Editor
Format:	Documentary
Project Length:	Five minutes including titles
Delivery Date:	One month from today
Audience:	Everyone in the community
Venue:	City Hall meeting room
Delivery Format:	Mini DV (Digital Video) Tape
Special Instructions:	• Use at least one interview • Use both interior and exterior locations • Identify 5 examples of poor water management • Present 3 recommendations for water conservation
Assessment:	Attached rubric

The Completed Form

Once the form is complete, it can be handed out to students as an outline of the filmmaking project.

Ideas Change

After all this decision making and brainstorming into what the project will look like is complete, I have some unsettling news. Ideas change. This is one of the most fundamental aspects of filmmaking.

What we think is a perfectly defined filmmaking project seems to transform and improve as ideas are generated and opportunities discovered. At every step of the filmmaking process, change happens, and it can be one of the most frustrating and rewarding experiences of making a movie.

Those filmmakers who stubbornly cling to old ideas and plans because they have been 'decided' or 'agreed upon' risk losing the remarkable opportunities for insight into both the subject they are exploring and the creative process itself.

Ideas are for moving you forward, not holding you back. They take you from where you have been to where you are going. As you move forward, your horizon changes, and that which you could not see a few moments before now informs your very next step.

Let go. Let your ideas change.

9: Developing Ideas

Now the fun begins. This stage of the filmmaking process is about asking questions, unleashing imagination, and using the power of research to strengthen and support the filmmaker's voice.

Once the filmmaker has a concept for a story, but before it is written down in a Script or Shot List, it is time to develop ideas of what the film could be about and how those ideas might be expressed. It is a process of investigation and questioning which leads to more investigation and further questioning. The challenge of this part of the filmmaking process is to let yourself go on an idea-generating adventure without an immediate concern for justification and logic. This means giving yourself permission to ignore, for now, the ramifications that each decision may bring.

This is not about editing, or asking how we would get a particular shot, or how we would get a particular resource that we think we need. This is also not about worrying if the ideas make perfect sense…yet. This is about the unabashed excitement of dreaming. It is the glorious 'what if' stage.

Minds beg to ask questions. We ask questions all the time. I wonder how this works? I wonder why that person is the way he or she is? I wonder what that song means? I wonder how that artist made that work? Developing ideas is often more about asking questions rather than deciding on answers.

Anyone who has worked with young people knows that their unbridled imagination constantly surprises us in the sheer volume of ideas, scope, and originality. And as well as imagination, young people have a deep well of questioning that they can, when motivated, draw upon. This is the exciting potential of this step: to harness that passionate imagination with focused questioning and exploration in an attempt to clarify what they

"An old thing becomes new if you detach it from what usually surrounds it."
Robert Bresson

want to communicate. In this process, we have an opportunity for students to develop their original ideas.

To do this, we must first create a safe arena for the discussion of these ideas. I say safe because it is often unsafe to tell others your ideas. We learn early in life that the rewards for new ideas are sometimes laughter, ridicule and isolation. Unfortunately, this is usually reinforced throughout our lives. We refrain from joining in discussions with family, friends and business and professional colleagues because we're afraid the other person or group of people might dismiss or ridicule our own fresh new ideas. We learn to protect ourselves from public humiliation by suppressing our desire to contribute ideas. What a shame.

Filmmaking provides us with the opportunity to create a more positive experience of exploring, announcing and valuing our ideas.

Do you remember looking into the night sky, at all the random twinkling lights, and thinking that they were just a lot of individual stars? Did someone point Orion's Belt out to you, or the Little Dipper's outline? Could you ever look at the sky again without searching for and recognizing those constellations?

Developing new ideas is like looking at that sky full of stars. Ideas are all around us in all aspects of life, but they wait for us to imagine, make connections and create something new. Developing new ideas is like playing connect the dots. Apparently random dots on a page are joined together to become an image, and apparently random bits of information in our minds are joined to form ideas.

Brainstorming

Brainstorming can be part of the process that enables these new constellations of ideas to be conceived, identified and recorded. Brainstorming is a fun, necessary, and very creative component of the filmmaking process.

Although there are no rules to brainstorming, here are a few guidelines to help make the most out of the session. Students can:

- Begin with a main idea.
- Associate images with this idea.
- Think of references to the main idea, subject or even the main word.
- Suggest ideas on how to explore these words and subjects further.
- Push the ideas as far as possible, no matter how wild.
- Prevent criticism or evaluations from occurring during the session. (Remember what we said about suppressing ideas.)
- Keep a record on paper, audio or video of the ideas that were generated.
- Set a time limit.
- Have fun.

Brainstorming can be facilitated by the teacher in a whole class session, or it can be carried out in small groups or by individuals.

Teacher-led sessions have the advantage of input from a large number of individuals, and the most divergent ideas. This can also be a disadvantage when the loudest or boldest voices obscure the creative but quiet ones.

I have found success working with small groups of five or six students at a time. I let them make all the decisions about what to record, and I let them do the recording. My role is to pay attention to their brainstorming direction and to help them ask questions about their own project. My goal is to have them discover that there are many possible ideas and many directions of exploration that can exist based on their central idea. I explain to students that this stage of filmmaking is not about being locked into decisions; it is about creating arenas of inquiry.

Another approach, and this exercise can happen before the small group or teacher-led session, is to have individuals brainstorm independently. Sometimes it is productive to set a short time limit of about five or ten minutes, and then spinning off the central

"An actor entering through the door, you've got nothing. But if he enters through the window, you've got a situation."
Billy Wilder

idea have them write down as many ideas as they can think of, on one page, just to get their stream of consciousness going. In fact, this whole exercise of an idea generating itself may lead into discussions about ideas and creativity, and how new ideas are created.

Mind Mapping

When we explore possible directions for our films, Linda and I sometimes get overwhelmed with the array of ideas and possibilities that have been generated during the brainstorming process. A method we frequently use to organize and communicate all of those ideas is to mind map. In fact, we often combine the two and mind map as we brainstorm.

For *Smoke*, Linda was interested in exploring memory. But when she began thinking of how she was going to write it, she was fascinated for some reason by the white smoke billowing from the top of the giant stacks at the local hospital. What is the connection? She did not know, but she believed there might be one.

So Linda started exploring smoke, and started writing down images that relate to smoke: smoke, drifting, cigarettes, smoked salmon, fire, eyes filled with tears, campfires. It was a way to invite new images and ideas into her story without worrying if they were the right ones. She then did the same for memory, life and death. This is what the mind mapping looked like.

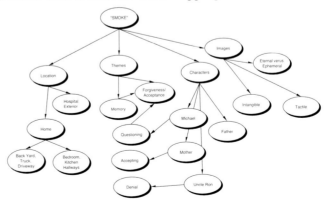

Below is a portion of a mind map that was produced by grade six girls in brainstorming their film *Friends*. It began with dividing their ideas into two groups, one for ideas about the story, the other for ideas about the characters. It eventually included strands that explored location ideas, wardrobe ideas, and more story details and possibilities. It also seems much more organized than ours!

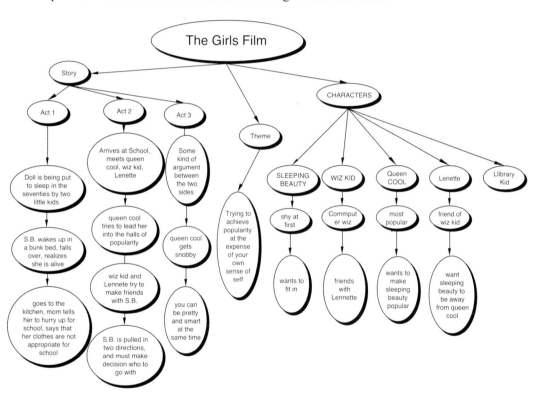

Both of the examples were produced using software called Inspiration™. Inspiration™, and the new product they have released for younger students called Kidspiration™, offer a great way to combine brainstorming and mind mapping at once. I do not work for or get paid to promote Inspiration™, so I can say that I have been using it for nearly ten years and it is still my favourite mind mapping software for my own projects and for working with students. Filmmaking is about working with sequences, and I find that early on in the filmmaking process organizing ideas into visual groupings really helps filmmakers begin to 'see' how their film will take shape.

Once you have finished brainstorming the project visually, Inspiration enables you to present the information in an outline view. I find that this is another great way of showing students how the unstructured process of brainstorming ideas leads into a structured outline, which can develop into a Shot List or Script. One of the great things about this process is that you can print off copies at the end of the session, or post it on a web site, and everyone has a record of the ideas and strands that were generated.

Do We Need Parameters?

One of the most challenging aspects of filmmaking in the classroom is creating projects that can be developed in the time allowed and with the resources at hand. I say this because what I often encounter is a desire by students to film the next sequel to Star Wars within the time frame of a fifty-minute class.

It is impossible for me to generalize what is and is not possible within the framework of classroom instruction. I have been confused when relatively simple exercises cause frustration and then pleasantly amazed to see extremely ambitious projects executed wonderfully.

I think the right number of parameters for a project is a flexible equation consisting of an instructor's own personal experience with video production, the grade and experience levels of the students, and the time and resources available. More than once, I have had to narrow the scope of a project in order for it to come to completion. It was necessary so that students could see a finished product of their efforts and experience that success.

"If it can be written, or thought, it can be filmed."
Stanley Kubrick

Having said that, I will contradict myself and say that if students understand the parameters of the project but still want to try something that is ambitious in terms of resources or time, then I look forward to seeing them surprise me. I do not want to extinguish any passion for learning that has been ignited, but I would have them sit down with me after they have researched it more and convince me that they can do it within the time available.

As with many other aspects of filmmaking, flexibility is important, and the ability to re-assess and redefine projects midstream is a great skill for students to have opportunities to develop.

Time to Develop Ideas

My wife Linda is a screenwriter. She goes for walks, plays with our daughters, folds socks, prepares dinner, and gardens, but all the while she is writing. She may not have paper and pen at hand, but she is writing. This is because the way she develops her ideas is by allowing herself time. Time to mull. She allows her ideas to interact with the rest of her life. Often the place where breakthroughs occur is at the intersection of concentrating on one idea and the tangential thinking that is brought into action from another, often-unrelated source. And this takes time. It is also important to explore with students this concept that ideas sometimes require time, reflection and distance in order to manifest.

The challenge of providing this time and contemplation in the classroom can be perplexing. How do we encourage and dedicate time to develop creative ideas for our projects in an already time-crunched day (year) of instruction?

One suggestion is for this to be done outside the classroom, by way of idea journals. These could be both ongoing journals of the production at hand, as well as a place to record thoughts for other filmmaking projects they may want to explore in the future. In my

"Comic ideas are cheap but ideas that flower, that develop into something are not so easy to find. It's laborious to plot out things; when you get that idea you tend to rush ahead too rapidly and you force the ending."
Woody Allen

experience with journals, the process of putting down questions, and the attentive focus that comes with it, allows for answers to come from everyday life and to appear on the page.

In a frenzied, fast-paced, instant email, 24/7, overnight delivery world, it seems important to remind students that breakthrough ideas are not always delivered overnight or at the push of a button, and that sometimes the quickest way to reach those breakthroughs is to take your time.

Research

One of the great things about filmmaking is research. Why? Because you encounter things you never knew existed. You are pushed into discovering new worlds. As a writer or director, I investigate stories, characters, geography, music, cultures and languages that I never knew existed. I research so that I am able to understand my subject and make informed choices in my script and in my filming.

Linda is currently working on a screenplay in which one of her characters works with autistic adults. To better understand the character and to make more truthful choices for that character's world, she is actively involved with research. She is on the Internet, researching autism on web sites and reading journals. She visits group homes. Her two brothers both work with autistic adults; through interviews she asks questions of them as if asking her own invented characters. And she will repeat this research for each of the different characters in her screenplay.

Every question is a door, and each piece of research is a room that opens up behind it. And every room that is explored contains more doors. And so she goes, further on this magical journey into the unknown, fuelling investigation with curiosity. And as she discovers real-life details of her imagined idea, she brings it back to the screenplay, and her research defines what ultimately her script and the film will be about. "Research continually informs my script," Linda says. Her mentor script editor John B. Frizzell puts it this way, "Research gives authority of voice."

Aristotle said, "For the purpose of story, a convincing impossibility is preferable to an unconvincing possibility." It comes down to this: know of what you speak!

Students can relate to this. Ask them if they can recall watching a movie or television program where they or their friends groaned, "That would never happen!" "As if." "Yeah right." What happened? The filmmaker portrayed an unconvincing possibility and the kids simply did not buy it. They were taken out of the believability of the movie because they perceived what they saw as false. Do they want this to happen with their own films? How can it be prevented? The answer is to take their research and integrate it into the framework and substance of their project.

The great thing about students researching information for their films is that it fosters confidence in their ability to answer the question: "How do I find out about something?"

I mentioned earlier the story of Marie. Here was a grade three student, wanting to be involved in a film, *The Princess and the Street Kid*, and needing to answer the question, "Were there sports in the Medieval Ages?" in order to become part of that film. Outside of school time, she researched books at the library, asked her parents questions, researched sites on the Web, and then came back to me with two pages of handwritten facts about horseback riding, jousting, archery, swordsmanship, and other knightly games. These facts supported her idea and argument that she should be William Tell. I love to see passion driving learning!

Another girl in the same project, Juliana, was focused on creating the costumes and sets. Off she went to the library, on the Web, into magazines—collecting images of princesses, princes and castles. She asked her parents about castles that they had photographed in Europe and then brought her research and ideas back to the other students.

"Were the roads cobblestone back then, Mr. Theodosakis?" "I don't know," I said, "What do you think?" "I don't know," she replied, "I'll have to research." Bingo!

I have seen students at all grade levels push and develop their research skills as they work on their filmmaking projects. They transform this investigation and filtering of the data that is all around them into an understanding of their subject. And all this research is passionately driven by their desire to make their movie.

Ideas Change

As the brainstorming, mind mapping, mulling and research bring forth fresh new ideas and new insights, the screenwriter refines the script and the filmmaker refines the project. And to do this, ideas must be allowed to change.

I have seen Linda write for days on a scene, and then delete it all, shrugging it off because it did not fit with the refined direction of the script. I have seen her delete entire sequences because her research had brought forward new, interesting choices and information. Though it is sometimes painful to throw away the work that you imagined complete, it re-enforces the fact that writing (and filmmaking) is a process, and the ability and courage to change your ideas and revise your work rewards you with a stronger, more articulated screenplay and film.

One of the changes in writing Linda refers to is "The Left Turn." It's that drastic change in direction that the writing and the research takes you in, despite your objections, and despite your insistence that you thought you knew what it was you were writing about. The truth is that left turns happen, and it is harder to not take them than it is to take them. When you allow yourself to take left turns and see what is around the corner, you are affirming your willingness to change, to learn, and to discover.

Change in the developing ideas stage is more than just

acceptable; it is critical for ensuring that our energies at every subsequent stage will be best utilized.

A common obstacle I have encountered is the reluctance of students to change their minds once they have decided on their original idea. It may be that this is part of a larger issue in our society of not recognizing and rewarding process and failure. There is so much pressure in life to get things right the first time, for students and adults alike, that we exclude failure as part of the process of discovery. Nobody wants to be wrong. And yet, when we enter the world outside the classroom, success is often the result of experimenting, learning from our mistakes, re-aligning ourselves and experimenting again. It is a process of continual learning where we increase our abilities and experience as we strive higher. We need to show students that success outside the classroom is often about reaching a mark, not getting one.

Students must realize that their ideas don't change because they were wrong, but because they have learned something. They have some new piece of information that they did not have at the time they created their original idea. Furthermore, if they had not come up with their original idea, they probably would have never uncovered the newer idea. There are no right or wrong ideas, only insights, and these insights are part of a continuum that leads us on a never-ending journey of exploration and discovery.

10: Making the Pitch

```
INT. MOVIE STUDIO OFFICE - DAY
A large, nicely furnished studio executive's office.
Framed movie posters line the wall. Behind a large
wood desk, an older man with a cigar is sitting in
a large padded leather chair. He looks up and sees a
single figure, a filmmaker, twirling his fedora.

                    STUDIO EXECUTIVE
          Scram, kid. I'm busy.

                    FILMMAKER
          Please, Mr. Studio Executive, I know
          you'll love this story. It's going to
          make a great movie.

                    STUDIO EXECUTIVE
          All right, all right, I'll give you two
          minutes. What's your pitch?
```

"I am a sensitive writer, actor and director. Talking business disgusts me. If you want to talk business, call my disgusting personal manager."
Sylvester Stallone

We've seen this cliché unfold in countless Hollywood films that look at how movies come to be. A busy studio executive waits patiently and the filmmaker begins. The filmmaker's goal is to passionately describe the story, engage his listener and convince him to take a chance and make the movie. This is pitching—describing your story to someone in the most exciting way possible so that they will want to support or be involved with your project.

Although I personally have never had to pitch to Hollywood studio executives and endure the smell of cigars, I do continually pitch my projects. When I am developing a film, I pitch actors and hope that my description of both the characters and the project captures their imagination and makes them want to be involved, or at least to ask me more questions.

The same goes for my crew. If there is a camera operator or sound technician that I would love to work with, I will pitch my story to them. And I will pitch my idea to broadcasters, distributors and financing groups.

The truth is, I am always pitching. Sometimes people who are not in the film industry will ask me what my film is about. When I tell them the story, what I am really doing is pitching to my audience, and I judge by their response if the story has connected with them or not.

If they fall asleep, I know I have to change my pitch, or perhaps even change my project. But if I can engage them and excite them, and they genuinely want to know more, then I know I am on the right track. Filmmaking is about communicating ideas.

This part of the filmmaking process is about the oral communication of ideas and the exciting possibilities embedded within. It is an opportunity for students to develop oral presentation skills, and an opportunity for them to learn about and experience how to deliver clear, concise, distilled information that provides an abbreviated but engaging experience to their audience.

Developing Oral Presentation Skills

Regardless of whether our students grow up to be filmmakers or not, they will find themselves with a need for good oral presentation skills. They will need to be able to have great pitching skills. As an exercise, ask students if they have ever pitched.

Has there ever been an occasion when they: Asked if they could stay up late? Asked to borrow twenty bucks? Asked to borrow a friend's bike? Pleaded to go to a movie? Begged their parents to do something for them? Asked their teacher to extend the report deadline? or, Have they ever asked someone out on a date?

Are the occasions mentioned above examples of pitching? Of course. They are all about convincing others about the benefits or validity of a particular idea. Success with each of those goals depends on the ability to engage, entertain and reassure.

But if we go past the need to help students pitch themselves for dates, where else does practice in pitching pay off to the student? It may be to pitch themselves in a job interview, in presenting their ideas in work environments, or in speaking out and leading change in their organizations and communities.

As a society, we need people in our communities who can express themselves articulately. We need people who will feel comfortable speaking to others, sharing ideas and introducing new thinking.

The fact is we live in a world where people pitch each other every single day. While the communication of our ideas to others may not resemble the formal pitch as in the Hollywood example, we can still recognize that, as human beings, we are constantly trying to sell our ideas to others. Instead of pitching, we call it suggesting, influencing, advising, advertising, bragging, selling, offering, recommending and proposing. But the goal is the same—to excite your audience about your idea in order to gain their support.

The reality of life is that we spend a lot of our day speaking and listening to others. We might even agree that we spend more time speaking and listening to each other than we do reading and writing to each other.

The question is, do schools put the emphasis on teaching students speaking and listening skills or on reading and writing skills? If part of education's goal is to prepare students with real-world skills, then perhaps the oral presentations that are part of filmmaking can help meet that goal.

Pitching to the Teacher

Imagine a teacher as the studio executive, minus the cigar,

"Apart from technical considerations, which is something that you learn over a period of time and experience, I think the ability to tell a story is of vital importance. I think the guy who can sit in a room and tell a story to people, grab their interest and hold their interest—that's the first step. To know what makes a story hold, too. How to set up a problem, how to set up a situation, how to set up conflict, how to create interest in a character."
Vincent Sherman

of course. After students brainstorm projects and research ideas, invite them to pitch the studio executive (the teacher).

In *The Director in the Classroom* workshops, I have participants break off into small groups and start generating ideas relating to their project. When they feel they have a story and a plan on how to shoot the film, I invite them to come up in their small groups and to pitch me.

What I want to see is if their idea for the film is in line with what was asked for in the workshop assignment. I also want to see that they have a clear understanding of what they are going to set off to shoot. If they're on track, I compliment them and send them off on the next step in the filmmaking process.

If their ideas are off track, or if they appear unclear of what they are going to explore, then I propose questions for them to consider to help them revisit the goals of the assignment and to help them get back on track.

The benefit of pitching to the teacher is that it provides students a safe environment to experiment with the process of oral communication. Both individually and in small groups, these sessions could form an important introduction to the complex world of telling people what you want to say.

Pitching to the teacher can also be integrated into the classroom filmmaking process. Much like the movie studio executive who invests in the film by giving the filmmaker the resources needed to make the movie, so too can the teacher be the one who releases resources, information and support. When students pitch their ideas, when they come to you with their story, you can say, "Yes, you have demonstrated that you know 'what' your film is going to be about." "Congratulations." "Now on to the next stage."

Later, after they have completed Storyboards and Shot Lists, they can pitch once more, demonstrating 'how' they are going to make it happen. Some teachers I have talked to allow the video cameras and other equipment to go out only after students have successfully demonstrated, through their second pitch and their accompanying materials, that they have a good plan to realize their desired footage.

Teachers do this because they have seen students frustrated by trying to shoot undeveloped projects. Let us also argue the opposite: that we learn best by doing and that trying to shoot an undeveloped idea may be the best way to teach the importance of all that planning. The approach is up to you.

As teachers are more sympathetic to hearing pitches than studio executives, it is usually a rewarding part of the process for all involved. Have fun!

Pitching to Each Other

As well as pitching to the teacher, students can pitch to each other. Perhaps the filmmaking assignment requires groups of four or five students. How are groups assigned? Are there opportunities for students to pitch each other? Perhaps it is about looking for actors or crew to help them make their movie? Without making it competitive, is there an opportunity for student-to-student pitching that can be investigated?

One possibility is looking at the idea of listening. Listening, as we said earlier, is what we do much of our lives; perhaps some students are developing oral presentation skills while others are developing listening skills. Perhaps students who are being pitched to can come up with one or two questions to ask the presenter based on their listening to the pitch. These questions may even help the presenter clarify to himself or herself what the project is about or how they intend to show it.

An exercise in listening may be appropriate to explore the relationship between how we speak and how we listen. When I work with actors, we often warm up with listening exercises. Acting should really be called 'reacting' because really great actors react to the other characters on the set. They don't come with a pre-rehearsed delivery of lines. They listen intently to each other and let the energy, emotion and actions of the other actor affect, infect, and inform their reaction, usually using the words of the script. If you want to really enjoy reading and learning about how great actors and great directors work together, I highly recommend reading *Directing Actors* by Judith Weston, a truly amazing book.

Here's an exercise Judith uses in her workshop. Two (or more) people sit facing each other. One person begins to tell a story. They say only one word, then the other person says only one word, and so it goes, back and forth, each person advancing the words into sentences and instantaneously inventing characters and situations. The goal is to keep the story going until someone loses concentration or cracks up laughing.

Try it. This fun exercise demonstrates the importance of hanging onto every word the other person says, and it illustrates how conversations, when reduced to such absurd exchanges, depend so much on listening to each other. Another benefit of students pitching each other may be examining how the pitch itself is delivered.

Is there a perceived difference in a pitch that is delivered loud and fast versus one that is whispered and reserved? Is there an ideal volume, energy level or frame of mind in which pitches should be delivered? Is eye contact with your audience important? Is it better to read off a paper or to memorize it and recite it by memory? Is listening to your audience's reaction to the pitch important? And most importantly, what have students learned in pitching and what would they change or refine for next time?

Pitching Outside the Classroom

Let's say a filmmaking project is described as follows:

The assignment is to produce a five-minute video that looks at one kind of multicultural experience that exists in our community and to go to that place, film it, bring it back, edit it and present the movie to the class.

Perhaps the film assignment must answer the question: Why is it important that we recognize different cultures in our community?

Suppose one student wishes to answer the assignment by looking at the questions through the context of a local Japanese restaurant. They must first find out which restaurants in their community are Japanese and then find out where they are, what their phone numbers are, and perhaps when they are open. All of this might come from a little research in the phone directory. So, they find the information, now they have to ask about permission to shoot there.

They might phone or ideally go in person and talk to the owner about what they are doing. There, in this Japanese restaurant, the student will explain (pitch) to the owner:

- What they are doing. (Producing a video report for school.)
- Why they are doing it. (To look at multiculturalism in the community.)
- How they are doing it. (Through short interviews with people about their business and themselves.)

All this may be scary, but it will accomplish a couple of goals. First, it will help exercise clear oral communication skills, and secondly, it will take the student out of the classroom and into the community.

One of the goals that was talked about in the first part of this book was building bridges. Here is a great chance for the student and school to build a bridge to their community and for the community to build bridges to the school.

Hopefully the Japanese restaurant owner will be happy to help out and then they can move on to scheduling questions. But what if he says no. What if he says, "Sorry, I'm too busy." Here is a great chance for listening and comprehension skills:

- Why was the request denied?
- What problems did the owner have that the student had not thought of?

- What other information did the owner require?
- Could the obstacle be overcome and the owner revisited?
- And most importantly, how would you change your pitch next time?

Cherie Hansen is a teacher who shared with me an experience from her grade ten classroom. They wanted to shoot part of their video at a very upscale waterfront hotel. They were originally thinking of trying to just 'steal' the shot, without permission. Hansen persuaded the group to pitch their idea to the hotel's manager. After much hesitation, the group called up the hotel, asked to speak to the manager, and set up an appointment for a meeting to explain their school project in person.

The day of the meeting arrived. They went down to the hotel, met with the manager; and were surprised at the results. The manager welcomed them with open arms. He provided them a special room to work out of, access to the facilities and the services of their staff. Filming went well and upon completion of the project, the teacher received a letter from the hotel manager saying how well behaved the students were in the hotel. He also said that the hotel was pleased to be part of the students' learning and that they were welcome back anytime.

Were any lifelong, real skills learned here? Were any revelations discovered of what can be achieved through etiquette and orderliness? Were there any connections made to how businesses work in the real world? Was there a real person behind the faceless Manager nameplate sign on the office door? Can students get support from their community if they ask for it? Will the students view the world in a slightly different way? Absolutely!

Ideas Change

As I mentioned earlier, when I tell someone my idea for a project I try to be constantly aware of their response, both in their body language and in the questions that they ask.

With each pitch, there is a continual refinement of the ideas, the delivery, the order with which the information is revealed, the pauses—in short, the total experience of how the communication is delivered.

The lessons students learn from each pitch, what went well or what went wrong, may find themselves documented in a notebook, or scratched on a piece of paper, or they might become intuitive changes that are brought instinctively to the next presentation. Regardless, learning from each pitch is about discovering how ideas change.

After pitching to the teacher, to each other, and to others outside the school, students discover better ways to tell their stories, and better stories to tell.

Ideas change, and again, it's about recognizing that it's all about a process that seeks to help clarify and articulate exactly what each unique filmmaker desires to say.

The lessons learned in pitching, like the other stages of filmmaking, are generously there to help students become successful communicators of their own ideas.

11: The Script

In theatre they say, "If it's not on the page, it's not on the stage." The same applies to filmmaking. The details of a good production originate from the fingertips of the writer, and they are communicated through the words and images of the screenplay.

Screenplays are magical documents. They articulate a vision of the finished film with all its characters, environments and action. All the details of what writers 'see' in their heads are presented and unravelled in a linear fashion from beginning to end.

On the pages of the screenplay, writers reveal information that they have researched and then they present that information through a series of detailed scenes. Each scene's goal is to advance the conflict, the characters or the story. Great scenes advance all of the elements simultaneously. Scenes combine to form sequences, sequences combine to become acts, and acts combine to become films.

Screenplays or 'scripts' are sometimes referred to as blueprints. I like using blueprints as an analogy, because scripts do provide the foundation on which the film is 'constructed.'

Scripts describe the places and events that have yet to be recorded or acted out. This is one of the benefits of using screenwriting in the classroom: it develops a fluency of working with visioning tools. Students create scripts as a method of communicating ideas of what they intend to create, and they must seek to articulate as many of the details as possible to illustrate their intangible world.

"The most ordinary word, when put into place, suddenly acquires brilliance. That is the brilliance with which your images must shine."
Robert Bresson

Developing Writing Skills

Another benefit of developing screenplays in the classroom is that it fosters the development of basic practical and creative writing skills.

When students create the written document that describes what it is they want to show, they are experimenting with communicating their creative ideas through rich descriptive language.

In the same way that pitching offered an environment for developing oral presentation skills, this part of the filmmaking process, the organization and transformation of words into screenplays, offers opportunities to develop practical and creative writing skills.

Current articles in education journals and studies argue for increased competency in basic writing skills. Filmmaking addresses this need. The creative act of writing a screenplay brings with it a responsibility to develop spelling, grammar, composition, structure and formatting skills. Regardless if the script is being delivered to the teacher in the classroom or a Hollywood executive, writing disciplines must be maintained.

- It should be free of spelling errors.
- It should be free of grammatical errors.
- It should have consistent tabs and indents that adhere to an agreed-upon format.
- It should be well constructed.

These practical writing skills can become one component in the discussion of the assessment of the finished project.

More challenging and equally important is the opportunity to develop the creative thinking that goes with creative writing. Are original ideas presented? How are they presented? Are students experimenting with characters, locations and action? Are scenes well constructed? Are they individual events? Are they connected?

The mechanical and creative processes combine to form the words of the screenplay. The pages of the screenplay are presented in a format that is standard throughout the movie industry.

Here is an example from our film, *Smoke*:

```
EXT. STREET OUTSIDE HOSPITAL — AFTERNOON
MICHAEL DALEMAN, an eight-year-old boy dressed in
poor but clean clothes and wearing an outdated
pack sack, looks up at a large smoke stack billow-
ing white smoke on top of a small town hospital.
JORDAN and TYLER, two ten-year-old boys, approach
Michael.
                    TYLER
Hi Michael
They elbow one another and join Michael looking up
at the smoke stack. Tyler says teasingly...


                    TYLER
        ...That's where they burn parts of
        people.


Michael turns to him, wide eyed.


                    TYLER
        There's a big fire-furnace in the
        basement where they burn 'em.


JORDAN joins in the teasing.
```

_____

This format explains where the action takes place, which characters are involved, what they are saying to each other, and what they are all doing. More examples of screenplay format are available on the attached CD and at the website <_www. thedirectorintheclassroom.com_>.

Exploring Language

When Linda sits in front of her computer and writes a script, she creates a series of images, and she paints those images

"For me, writing is just part of the directing process. The writing is one draft, the shooting is the next draft, and the editing is the last draft."
James Cameron

with words. Screenwriting brings out students' writing skills by encouraging them to paint images with words.

When a distributor, a broadcaster, or an actor somewhere around the world reads Linda's script, they may not have the familiarity of place that Linda has, and so she, as a screenwriter, must describe to them her interpretation of that distinct piece of geography and convey to the reader that specific sense of place.

The screenplay *Smoke* takes place in the Okanagan Valley of British Columbia. One of the scenes is about Michael's memory of an ice fishing expedition.

How do you describe the campsite, the frozen lake, and the terrain of the nearby mountains? What are the physical specifics of ice fishing? What specific details could be included to bring the location to life for someone who has not been there? How do you use words to describe place? How do you describe to someone what he or she would see, in detail, if they too could stand where you have stood?

These are the challenges facing the screenwriter. There is the opportunity for students to exercise the process of imagining, visualizing, interpreting and communicating what they see, both in real life and in the imagined. This is about exploring how you can use words to communicate and connect with others.

The same question applies to describing the characters and events throughout the story, "How do you show it with words?"

Let's look at characters. How do you use words to describe a person? How would you describe them physically? Mentally? Socially? What kinds of things do they do? How do they speak? And what does how they speak and what they do tell us about what kind of person they are?

Let's go into a classroom.

I worked with a group of grade six girls who were creating a dramatic story for a class project. The girls' movie explored the theme of peer pressure at school. Their script started off in one character's bedroom, on an afternoon when three of her friends have joined her at her home.

As they worked on the script, I asked the girls to describe what they saw in that character's room.

- What kind of furniture did she have?
- What posters were on her walls?
- Were her clothes all hung up in her wardrobe or all over the floor? Does it matter?
- What does that tell us about the character?
- What about her friends, did they think they were sitting near her, or were they far?
- Were they glad to be there, or were they uncomfortable?

This is what we do in screenwriting, we investigate. As the writer, we consider everything, ask questions, make decisions, and tell a specific story using the characters, the places and the events that we have selected.

Storytelling

Filmmaking is about telling stories. True stories, make-believe stories, and sometimes made-up stories that are truer than truth itself.

Documentaries and fiction films, though different in approach, give audiences something identical, the storytelling experience. We meet characters, visit new worlds and observe journeys.

When students make their own films, whether documentaries or fictional narrative, they become storytellers. By doing so, they begin to learn about the craft of storytelling itself.

I worked with a grade three class who had, not surprisingly, an abundance of things that they wanted to include in their fiction film. They had many stories to include about the characters, but there was no order to it. I put three pieces of paper on the board. At the tops I wrote Act 1, Act 2 and Act 3.

We used this opportunity to look at the storytelling structure

"Now in the shape of this thing, it is inevitable that you must design your incidents and your story shape to mount up. I always think the film shape is very much like the short story. Once it starts, you haven't time to let up. You must go right through, and your film must end on its highest note. It must never go over the curve. Once you have reached your high spot, then the film is stopped."
Alfred Hitchcock

itself. With giant post-it notes, we stuck their story ideas on the three sheets of paper, identifying where they belonged by simply asking the question: "Do you think this would happen at the beginning of the story, in the middle of the story, or at the end of the story?"

Although this approach may seem very basic, it became a successful introduction to exploring the three-act structure and the idea that stories can and usually do have a beginning, middle and an end. This is the essence of storytelling.

With high school students I like to suggest visiting <*www.adcritic.com*>. Here is a free resource and a fun way to explore thirty-second storytelling. On the site are hundreds of television commercials, many of them quite humourous, and many of them perfect examples of storytelling, albeit in such a short form.

One exercise, which begins acquainting students with the structure of story, is to select a commercial from that site, and to analyze it by writing a script for it. In other words, to deconstruct that commercial back from the finished product to what a script for it may have looked like.

By looking at their own scripts for the deconstructed commercial, students can investigate how scripts provide answers to questions, such as:

- Where does the story take place?
- Who is the hero?
- What is his or her quest?
- What are the obstacles of the journey?
- What is the resolution?
- How are the story events revealed?
- What is the turning point?

Now obviously not all commercials will be appropriate stories for deconstruction. Flowing pastorals that are backdrops for promoting nasal decongestants are not what I am talking about here. What I am suggesting is that commercials, the right commercials, can be a piece of familiar pop culture that students can relate to,

Development

and which they can analyze prior to beginning their own script-writing projects.

Mythic Structure

Why would grade six boys, inhabitants of a Nintendo world, be eager to study classical Greek mythology and literature? To make their own movie better, of course. I was "consulting" with a group of grade six boys who were making a video called 'The Y3K Bug.' It was their exploration of how too much technology could be a bad thing.

They knew they wanted their story to be about a technology-obsessed boy named Techno who becomes sucked into the World Wide Web. Trapped inside the web sites, he encounters the Y3K Bug, an evil computer bug, and must defeat the bug and then figure out a way to escape. They weren't sure what else they needed.

I asked the students if they had heard of Theseus and the Minotaur, and some of them had. I recounted the story of Theseus and invited them to point out any similarities they could think of to their story idea. They connected the World Wide Web to the Labyrinth, their Y3K Bug to the Minotaur, and their Techno to Theseus. Because they were passionate about making the best possible movie about a guy getting sucked into the world wide web, they not only listened to my recounting of the myth, but they were also able to draw connections of that story to their own. They were engaged.

They realized that their story might be more exciting if they could add obstacles for Techno to encounter in his journey. Studying Theseus and the Minotaur not only strengthened their screenplay and their film, but also their personal understanding of heroes, magical worlds, and the hero's journeys.

Ancient history comes alive, and is best understood when its relevance to the student's world is revealed.

"I think that nearly all stories can do with suspense. Even a love story can have it. We used to feel that suspense was saving someone from the scaffold, or something like that, but there is also the suspense of whether the man will get the girl. I really feel that suspense has to do largely with the audience's own desires or wishes."
Alfred Hitchcock

Documentary Scripts

When the filmmaking project is about creating a documentary, we have to look at another kind of a script format. Documentary scripts cannot anticipate what people will say, what they will do or what events will happen. They are about recording real events as opposed to recreating them. Documentary scripts can still be about storytelling, journeys, heroes and new worlds, but they portray those elements through the observation of actual people, places and events.

Here is a script page for my documentary, *Breaking Plates*. The description tends to describe a blend of what I would like for the story, what I think I will find, and what I hope will happen.

EXTERIOR. Busy Street City of Hania (Crete, Greece)
It is another busy day in downtown Hania. Noisy cars and motorcycles pass back and forth the Harhalis Cafe doors. Pedestrians walk by with groceries and bags, oblivious to the people inside the cafe.

The sign above the door reads "Cafenio Harhalis."
A man walks into the cafe and closes the door behind him.

INTERIOR Harhalis Cafe — Day
Musicians are gathered around the small cafe. Most are sitting at small wooden tables and are drinking coffee. In the kitchen of the cafe, the owner is boiling up more coffee and pouring it into tiny demitasse cups.

Two men are playing music.
One is playing Laouto and the other Lyra.
We listen to them for a while, then observe Georgio Tzimakis, music teacher.

He talks about his 70 years of teaching music, and
how folk music in Crete is changing, soon to be lost,
like other aspects of Cretan culture, to globalization
and progress.

When I went to Greece and filmed my music teacher, Georgio
Tzimakis, I had a strong idea of what I wanted to record in order
to tell the story. I recorded the café, the owner cooking up coffee
in the little kitchen, the musicians relaxing at tables along the wall
and the two musicians playing their folk music.

I was able to capture the details of that scene by using a
planning tool called a Shot List.

Shot Lists

Traditionally, the Shot List is a listing of the images that are
to be recorded by the film crew for a particular scene, location or
shooting day. The Shot List is most often created by the director,
working with the director of photography, based on the finished
screenplay. The objective is to fully understand what specific shots
must be photographed in order to tell the story of the scene.

The list will include information about what the shot is about
(what is the subject), what kind of shot it is (close-up, wide shot,
establishing shot, etc.), information about how the shot is photographed, (low angle, high angle, etc.), perhaps when, (day, night)
and usually where (interior, exterior, inside of a building, at the
park).

For the *Breaking Plates*, the Shot List looked like this:

Shot List ▪ ◻ ◻

Shot	Int/Ext	Description	Close-up (CU)
1	Ext.	Café. Traffic.	Wide
2	Ext.	Tilt down from sign to door, person enters	CU
3	Int.	Establishing shot of patrons at tables	Wide, Med CU
4	Int.	Owner making coffee	Med, CU
5	Int.	Two musicians playing	Med
6	Int.	Laouto player	Med, CU
7	Int.	Lyra Player	Med, CU
8	Int.	Details of Laouto (Large Bass Mandolin)	CU
9	Int.	Details of Lyra (3 String Violin)	CU
10	Int.	Tzimakis drinking coffee, listening to music	Med
11	Int.	Tzimakis Interview	CU
12	Int.	Details – coffee cup, his fingers drumming on the table	CU

Although the Shot List is, as we said, traditionally a planning tool, I mention it in this chapter devoted to screenplays for two reasons. First, if the thought of writing a screenplay is intimidating to students, a gentler introduction to scripts may begin with the construction of this kind of a Shot List. This document, like a screenplay, still answers the question, "What do you see?" and, "In what order do you see your images connected?" This applies to documentary and fiction films alike. Filmmaking is a visual medium and the key part of understanding it is to experiment with its visual language.

Secondly, there may not be time in your day, week, month or year of instruction to develop a full screenplay. This abbreviated format provides at least a basic written-down explanation of the images and the scenes that are required.

Having said this, I strongly urge investing time and energy into developing Shot Lists or Scripts. I cannot say this enough, because the more thought put into the filmmaking project at this stage, the more rewards and less disappointment will emerge as students continue along the filmmaking process. If it is not on the page, it is not on the stage.

Ideas Change

As with every step so far, the process of writing and experimenting with words leads to even more insights and awareness of the topic being examined. Once again, the articulation of ideas causes a refinement of what the film is about, and the changing drafts of the script also cause the project to adapt and react.

I was sitting in with a group of grade twelve students who were writing a script for a thirty-second commercial. The project addressed the tragedy of lives cut short from preventable driving accidents. The commercial aimed to marry a valedictorian speech with a eulogy. The goal was to create a speech that might be heard at both events, and which in alluding simultaneously to both life and death might emphasize the fragile line that separates each.

The stumbling block was the monologue itself. One group had written something which the other group felt was too somber for a valedictorian speech and the speech that the valedictorian group had written didn't feel right for the eulogy. There were defendants on both sides of the table of why the speeches had to be what they were, and that it would be impossible to change or combine them.

During that session, a young man in the corner put up his hand, and quietly said, "I've re-written something here. It's a little choppy, but I tried to combine both of them." He read it aloud and the words moved us all.

There were a few seconds of silence. He had succeeded in combining both versions. Writers from both groups started nodding their heads, and realized that, yes, it was possible to combine, and yes, it was possible to revise and to edit. They learned that words can be changed, dialogue can be changed, and that ideas can be changed. He was excited. The students were excited. There was a renewed passion for investigating the words and the work. Change is good.

12: Storyboarding

Pitching was all about developing oral presentation skills while articulating ideas. Screenplays and Shot Lists were about developing mechanical and creative writing skills while further articulating those ideas. Now we look at storyboarding, which enables students to develop visual presentation skills within the continuing process of examining, analyzing and refining the ideas once more.

Storyboards are comic book-like sketches of the different shots that make up the film. They indicate information about what the shot is about, where it takes place, what angles are suggested, what lighting is required and what movement, if any, the camera provides.

Storyboards may be highly detailed elaborate watercolours or simply drawn stick figures. They may be created by a professional storyboard artist, or by the director. Regardless of the finished quality of the Storyboard, what is ultimately important is not what the Storyboard is, but what it does.

The Storyboard is an important tool for transferring the vision that is inside the filmmaker's head into a tangible, shareable document. It opens up discussion of the story, and specifies what is to be filmed and how. It is this wonderful process of translating abstract concepts onto paper, of learning how to visually express one's vision to others, that makes storyboarding an important communicating tool for students.

Developing Visual Presentation Skills

We live on a planet where increasingly we communicate with each other through pictures and images rather than through the written and spoken word. We are living in a visual world and our children are part of it.

"So I started making drawings and paintings as the only other way I could imagine to communicate something of my vision; if I could get people to see these drawings, then at least something would get across."
Akira Kurosawa

"Well, I never look through the camera, you know. The cameraman knows me well enough to know what I want—and when in doubt, draw a rectangle and then draw the shot out for him. You see, the point is that you are, first of all, in a two-dimensional medium. Mustn't forget that. You have a rectangle to fill. Fill it. Compose it. I don't have to look through a camera for that."
Alfred Hitchcock

They look at television, movies, web sites, magazines, packaging, and take for granted that messages are continuously being sent to them through photographs, illustrations, colour, shapes, sizes, images, action, and movement. Unknowingly, they are interpreting those messages with an instinctual visual literacy.

I bought my daughter Matia a bike. It came in a box. Some Assembly Required. Three words that strike fear into the hearts of most parents. Sure enough, the written assembly instructions, though they used the English alphabet, stumped me. But by looking at the picture on the front of the box, we started putting the bike together.

At one point, I kept reading the instructions and could not figure out how it would possibly go together. Matia suggested that the instructions were wrong, and proceeded to show me, based on the cover photo, what I was doing wrong. She was right; the instructions were wrong. I had trusted the written word over the visual image.

Airlines have been able to reduce life-critical safety instructions into a three-fold colour brochure, which, through cartoon representations of passengers, airplanes and disasters, communicate to their audience what to do in case of an emergency. Regardless of what language you speak, you can still understand a visual message presented to you through pictures, images and graphics.

Visual instructions are everywhere. It is not always because we cannot read a language, but that we prefer a visual approach. "Let me show you what I mean," has become the marketers' mantra.

On the Web there are sites that use video and audio to show audiences how to do everything from navigating new software to repairing a leaky kitchen sink.

As we work increasingly with others in foreign countries, as speed of communication and instant feedback gives us shorter deadlines and instant decisions, perhaps we will see a new version of a global language, Esperanto 2.0, that is constructed from a visual alphabet. If a picture is worth a thousand words, then perhaps a whole alphabet of images might be appropriate for the United Nations of the Planet. But I digress.

For today's global inhabitants, some form of visual language is required. The use of storyboarding in filmmaking projects is about creating an environment of opportunity in which students can learn and experience that visual language.

Beyond making films, learning how to Storyboard is about experiencing another tool of communication that can be used in expressing ideas to others.

Today in business we see the use of visual presentations exploding. Simple-to-use presentation software makes it technically easy to produce a slide show or visual presentation.

What is required, however, is an understanding of the flow of ideas, the timing, and the critical order of revealing information that makes any communication medium powerful and meaningful. As with the other steps in filmmaking, the process of storyboarding enables students to develop effective, life-long communication skills.

Telling a Story With Pictures

Storyboarding is about telling a story with pictures. Filmmakers use Storyboards to communicate specific ideas and information to others in their industry.

Storyboards spark discussion and enhance communication. They facilitate the communication and evaluation of ideas at an early part of the filmmaking process to help anticipate problems and explore opportunities.

They help clarify the purpose of the individual scenes and of the entire movie.

"For Duel, the entire picture was storyboarded. I had the art director sketch the picture on a mural that arced around the motel room. It was an aerial view that showed all the scenes and the dead ends and the chases and all the exciting moments."
Steven Spielberg

Here is a Storyboard from the film, *Smoke*:

The Storyboard is a tool:

- For the director to communicate specific ideas to the production team.
- For the director, alone, to evaluate specific choices in how to best tell the story.
- To launch discussion with the director of photography about how each scene will be photographed.
- For communicating to the art department how much of

the background is seen, thus clarifying how much they have to prepare.

- For communicating to the assistant directors exactly which actors are in each shot so that they can schedule them accordingly.
- For communicating to the editor what the order of shots is so that potential storytelling or transition problems can be recognized and corrected before filming begins.
- For communicating to actors the relationship of one scene to another.

Storyboards provide information on characters, plot, setting, camera angles, camera movement, lighting ideas and other information. The director uses these images of visual information to explore and anticipate the production with their filmmaking team. By looking at them, they can see that each of the drawings answers the following questions.

- Who (or what) is the subject in this shot?
- Are we near or distant from the subject?
- Are we looking at the subject from eye level, from high above, or from below?
- Is the lens static or does it zoom in or out?
- Is the camera moving or is it static?
- What happens before and after that shot?
- What sets or locations are required?
- Are there any titles superimposed on the screen that give us additional information?

The reason that all these questions are asked and why it is important that they are answered is that filmmaking is very time consuming and very expensive. It brings together dozens or hundreds of trained professionals into a common project for a relatively short duration of time. When production is underway, logistical, equipment, and other resource problems delay production and prevent the filmmaker from creating the film. This is the dreaded over-budget, behind-schedule scenario we occasionally hear about. Storyboards help prevent some of

"The main purpose (of Storyboards) is to communicate to my cameraman and my crew the look I am trying to achieve, but I also do them to help myself because in the process of drawing I have to develop concrete images of the costumes, sets, the background—everything that's going to go into the frame."
Akira Kurosawa

these problems from rearing their ugly heads later on.

I have worked on films where the director has not taken the time to Storyboard. The films are still made, but there is an unnecessary confusion regarding what exactly is required, what exactly we see or do not see with each shot, and how we are going to shoot it.

More than once, I have seen art department staff prepare sets that never get seen, or find locations that are stunning, only to have a close-up used that could have been shot somewhere else, saving time or money.

Now as a director myself, I also change my mind and sometimes I do ask for more or less than I had planned for. But I must remember that every wall that is decorated, every street that is prepared, and every location that is added requires the talents, energies and resources of my team and of my budget.

Because we work with constraints of time and money, my goal is to focus my team's work on that which will show up on the screen. The result of reducing wasted resources is being able to re-allocate those resources towards something else that will help me make a better film. Concise instructions may translate into savings of time or money, and that may translate further into more rehearsal time, better equipment, better locations, or perhaps an additional day of shooting.

Here again is another benefit of Storyboards in the classroom filmmaking process. Because of the shortage of time, of equipment and of money in our learning institutions, there always seems to be a critical need to best utilize what resources we do have, whether it is a single camera in the school or a full media lab.

When students Storyboard their productions, they develop another life-long skill about learning how to critically evaluate their plans in order to stretch their resources.

Comic Books

One of the most fun and effective tools for exploring Storyboard concepts with students is to study comic books. Most of us are familiar with Batman, Spiderman and the hundreds of super heroes whose adventures have been chronicled in comic books. For today's students, this is a popular cultural medium with which most are familiar. Ask your students to come to class with their favourite comic book and see if that doesn't peak up their interest. Comics are great tools to learn about filmmaking because they are perfect examples of visual storytelling.

In an interview with film director Nicholas Ray, who filmed *Rebel Without a Cause* and many other great films, he stated that when he first came to Hollywood he would sit in late night cafés with film editors and look over Dick Tracy comics. They would look at how the story was told in pictures. They would dissect it and look at when close-ups or wide shots were used, or what type of composition and perspective to the background were used.

Comic book 'directors' use a visual language to enhance storytelling and to heighten the audience's involvement and appreciation of the story. Look at how a comic book reveals its story through a series of frames. It may start with a frame that shows a city skyline at night. Then a closer frame of a building with its lights on, in which some figures may be silhouetted inside. Then there is a frame that shows us those same shady characters inside the office, standing around a boardroom table, planning to overthrow the world. Then perhaps there will be a really close frame of a Top Secret document on a table. Then perhaps there is a frame of that same super hero crashing through the door, followed by a series of frames of everybody battling.

The sequence of the frames and the decision of when to use each one are all part of the process of deciding how best to tell the story with pictures.

In a classroom, comics can be a great jumping-off point as students prepare to storyboard their own projects. The variety of images, angles and moods found in comic pages serve as an

"I go right to the comic books—I get hundreds of them when I'm preparing these things. There's nothing better for color, framing, action or fun. They're just spectacular."
Joel Schumacher

introduction to thinking in terms of visual choices and exploring how students will visually unravel and reveal their story.

One approach in using comics as a tool for learning is to have students take a page from their favourite comic and deconstruct it. Beginning with the first image, or frame, consider the following questions.

Frame One:
- What is this frame about?
- Who is the subject of the frame?
- How close are we to the subject?
- How high are we compared to the subject?
- Where does this take place?
- Is there action in the frame?

These are just some of the questions that we can ask.

Drawing, Painting and Other Art Skills

When the great Japanese filmmaker Akira Kurosawa prepared Storyboards for his epic films like *Dreams*, *Ran* and *Kagemusha*, he painted elaborate watercolours that were rich with detail. As a filmmaker working with literally armies of people, he used these paintings as tools to communicate his vision of the film to his team. His films are rich in detail and his beautiful Storyboards now hang in museums and collections around the world. Although they are now considered masterpieces, they were created out of his genuine desire to clearly articulate his creative vision to others.

In the classroom, Storyboards are an opportunity for students to develop drawing, painting and other art skills. Storyboards can be simple or elaborate, in black and white or in colour, small or large, rough stick-figure sketches or polished detailed paintings.

They can also be a series of photographs. Some directors photograph small wooden art mannequins, those bendable figures

"I define certain kinds of ideas I want to explore within a certain framework. Very often I'll make little sketches or a brief Storyboard, thoughts or notes on three-by-five cards. I use these things, but unlike the novelist, who creates it out of his head, I go out then and struggle with people and places to form the film."
Ed Emshwiller

found in art supply houses, and use them as quick examples of where the actors are in relation to each other or to the frame.

Some directors use photographs as a storyboarding tool, and others use animation to give their Storyboards more action. In producing television commercials, it is common to produce an 'animatic.' An 'animatic' is simply an animated Storyboard. It shows the sketches for each intended shot, in sequential order, edited together with music and narration, and timed to the desired length of the proposed finished commercial. Some directors create video Storyboards by filming with digital video and trying things out inexpensively for themselves long before production begins.

Regardless of how elaborate Storyboards become, their reason for existence is to be a tool for enhancing communication and developing ideas. Regardless of the skill or technique involved to produce it, it must always answer the question, "What are we filming?"

Storyboards do not have to be complicated to be effective. I worked with a group of students who each produced a series of Storyboards for a project that they were working on. Many of them were quite elaborate, some were in colour and some were produced on a computer, but the Storyboard that was most useful for communicating the shot to the camera team ended up being one girl's very simple stick-figure pencil sketch.

It included all the elements of the shot. It showed how the action would unfold and in simple sketches achieved its purpose clearly. The sketch, which was almost laughed at by others in the class for its simplicity, turned out to be the most effective communication piece. A template for a Storyboard is on the CD and in the Appendix.

Developing Creativity

Storyboarding develops creativity in many ways. As well as developing painting, drawing and other art skills, storyboarding

"I always drew when I was a kid, I did cartoons because they were the most entertaining. It's easiest to impress people if you draw a funny picture. And I think that was a sort of passport through a lot of my early life. The only art training I had was in college, where I majored in Political Science. I took several art courses, some drawing classes and sculpture classes I'd never actually taken oil painting, any of those forms of art. And again, I was always criticized because I kept doing cartoons instead of more serious painting. My training has actually been fairly sloppy. I've been learning about art in retrospect. But I've always just kept my eyes open. Things that I like I am influenced by."
Terry Gilliam

"It starts with me from boards, and I work out the angles, I work out the perspectives, I work out the scene cuts from the dialogue and the action. I draw it all out—Storyboard it—as I go."
Bob Taylor

also develops creative thinking as to how the story will be revealed, how each scene will be constructed, and how the filming will be executed.

When we hear stories read to us, or when we ourselves read them, we see characters and worlds in our imagination. No two people see in their imagination a story illustrated in the exact same way. Storyboarding can be a method of examining this very fact: that we all look at stories and the world differently.

As a class exercise, consider using one or two lines of dialogue and description from a book and have students Storyboard it separately. The students will have different ideas and methods of how to illustrate that same story. And this is the whole point, that there does exist infinite possibilities of how to show a story, and because of this, there is no wrong way, only different approaches.

But by examining movies, comic books, commercials, and other Storyboards, students can enter into a discussion as to what they consider to be the most effective tools to work with, what other students consider valuable, and what visual grammar they might explore in the expression of their own films.

Developing Logic Skills

Storyboards are great tools for developing logic skills. Deciding how to sequence images to best reveal a story or explain an idea is another great benefit of using Storyboards.

Learning how to design and present ideas in a logical, storyboard form has great student benefits beyond the parameters of filmmaking itself.

Walt Disney used Storyboards as a tool for evaluating ideas for his animated and live action films, but he and his colleague Mike Vance also developed a process for business planning which they called 'displayed thinking.'

Increasingly, storyboarding is being used in mainstream business as a tool for business planning and modeling. PowerPoint™

presentations include an overview mode, which is really a Storyboard format of the presentation, with each slide represented as a frame, and each frame appearing in its relevant order. In fact, designing an excellent audio-visual presentation will benefit from concepts first developed as Storyboards.

For instance, let's say that you were designing a presentation for the Parents Advisory Committee with the goal to raise money for purchasing a video camera. Consider storyboarding what the night of the presentation might look like if it was to be filmed.

The first sketch may be simply a title that will eventually become a slide, overhead or presentation software graphic that says, "A Video Camera for the Classroom: A Presentation to the Parents Advisory Committee." The sketch represents where the title should go in respect to the entire presentation, and in this case, it belongs at the beginning.

The second sketch may be of a VCR/monitor on an AV cart with the note, "Play a few minutes of student-created videos." This sketch may represent the portion of the evening where examples of student filmmaking projects are presented.

The third sketch may be of a presenter in front of a screen, perhaps with notes that the bullets on screen will cover student benefits, why the camera is important and what other schools are doing.

And so it goes, as you imagine in a logical order how the night will proceed, how the information will flow, and how the ideas that you want to express will be presented to the audience. Then it will help to look at it, analyze it, and continually refine it until it becomes the final presentation.

Storyboarding enables you to look at the presentation of your idea as a series of logical sequences and helps you decide which order is the best possible order for communicating your ideas to others.

"*I try to visualize the script as far as I can, breaking each scene down into components, until I know exactly how I want to enter the scene, exit the scene, and everything in between.*"
Martin Scorsese

Pre-Production

Ideas Change

Once again, the process of exploring our ideas refines how our stories will be told. Storyboards are the intermediary step between words on paper and images on a screen. They are about giving words a shape, texture and mood, and giving shape to characters, location and action.

Creating storyboards is a method for students to create a dry run of the movie that audiences will eventually see. In doing so, students can pre-evaluate how their film will be composed, and decide how, where or if they want to introduce changes.

Ideas change, and storyboards help us understand why. It may be because we see creative alternatives to how we originally conceived the project. It may be because others can now see our vision and ask us questions and suggest ideas that reinforce or challenge our original ideas. It may be because the process of putting down ideas from start to finish reveals both problems and opportunities. Regardless, storyboarding makes for a more informed film and a more informed filmmaker.

 **Planning**

"Intellectuals solve problems; geniuses prevent them."
-Albert Einstein

The planning process of making movies is a very time consuming and exacting process. It requires patience, attention and articulation. This is one of the reasons why filmmaking is such a rewarding experience for students. The thinking that goes into preparation is what some people call 'hard fun.' For students, it is challenging but bearable because the energy they put into preparation results in the best possible movie they can make.

Although this chapter describes the planning process involved in both a 'professional' and student production, remember that nothing here is set in stone. Sometimes planning responsibilities change from department to department or between crew members. Every movie is, after all, unique.

I want to explore how the planning process usually works and then make some suggestions on how it can be incorporated into the classroom. Try some or all of these ideas as you design your own video projects, and experiment wildly. You will discover which ideas to include, which to omit, and which to invent.

Make a cup of coffee. Stretch your legs. Get ready. This is a big (but very fun) chapter. Planning is such a huge part of filmmaking that it is impossible to rush through it.

Developing Problem Solving, Logic, Analysis, Estimating, Budgeting, Scheduling and Visioning Skills

It is often said that filmmaking is problem solving. As a producer, one of my roles is to solve problems and ideally, it is to prevent them from occurring at all. This requires the development and maintenance of many skills including problem solving, logic, analysis, estimating, budgeting, scheduling and visioning, not to mention resourcefulness, good humour and patience!

"Movies are so expensive...You don't want to find yourself wasting everybody's time, walking around saying, "Maybe we should do this, maybe we should be over there, maybe we should do endless things."
Robert Benton

Most of my work as a producer and the majority of my work as a director is about planning. When you make a movie, there are so many details to consider, that planning becomes an intrinsic part of the whole process. This applies to the $100-million Hollywood epic as much as it does to the low budget or no budget student project. Regardless of the size of the project, planning is essential.

Here are some of the key steps in the planning process:

1. **Shooting Script**
   It begins by having a script that everyone agrees is ready to shoot. Not surprisingly, this is called the shooting script. Everyone knows that it still may change a bit.
2. **Script Breakdown**
   Determining what individual elements are required in order to film each scene, such as actors, sets, props, wardrobe, etc.
3. **Selecting Location**
   Deciding where exactly the physical filming will take place.
4. **Equipment**
5. **Refining the Team**
6. **Scheduling**
   Creating a Shooting Schedule. Deciding which scenes will be filmed on each day of the production.
7. **Budgeting**
   Creating a Budget. Allocating how much time is available for filming. Optional in student productions, but encouraged by yours truly.
8. **Problem Solving**
   Determining what shortfalls and obstacles arise from our application of the Schedule against the Budget and then solving them.
9. **Communicating to the Team**
   Distributing the final results of the breakdowns and schedules to the rest of the filmmaking team.
10. **Final Preparations**
    Conducting rehearsals.

Step 1. Shooting Script

A Shooting Script differs from a regular Script only in that it contains sequential reference numbers next to each scene description. This is done to facilitate the breakdown and scheduling process. Here is an example of the shooting script from our film, *Smoke*. The numbers on the left will identify these scenes throughout the entire planning, production and post-production phase.

```
3    EXT. ICE FISHING - DAY
Michael, Ron and Michael's father, Randy Daleman, an
older version of Ron, are ice fishing. Michael is having
fun as he and Randy fight to get a big one up through
a hole in the ice. It's early in the day but Randy
and Ron are both drinking. Michael is the centre of
attention as he pulls up the huge, fighting salmon.


4    EXT. MICHAEL'S  BACKYARD—AFTERNOON
     Ron's saying something but Michael is miles
away.
                         RON
          What're you doing?
                       MICHAEL
          Nothing.
```

Once a Script has been numbered, it becomes the Shooting Script. An alternative to the Script example above is to use a simple Shot List as shown below, which lacks the detail contained in a Shooting Script.

Shot	Location	Cast	CU
3	Ice Fishing Lake	Michael, Ron, Dad	CU
4	Michael's Backyard	Ron and Michael	Wide
...			

Step 2. Script Breakdown

The next step of the planning process begins with what is called a 'script breakdown.' This process is about going through the Shooting Script or the Shot List and extracting specific details. As a producer, I ask the question, "What do I need, exactly, to make this film?" The breakdown process provides me with the answer.

Filmmakers find it helpful to organize these details into categories, which conveniently correspond to the different departments on the film crew. The breakdown process results in a list of locations for the location department, a list of props for the prop department, a list of cast for the casting department and so on. Often the producer performs a preliminary breakdown during the development phase of the project, in order to give themselves some rough budgeting or scheduling ideas. Later, the department heads will work together to create a thorough breakdown document that their team will use to work from.

For example, on our current short film, *Smoke*, Linda and I look through the nine pages of script and identify the specific elements that are required in the different categories. Later, when our crew is assembled, we will revisit the breakdowns with them, take into account any script revisions, discuss ideas and revise them as necessary. Here are some of the breakdowns.

There will be a ***list of characters***, with a brief description:

SMOKE Cast Breakdown		
Character	**Age**	**Notes**
Michael	8	
Ron	45	Michael's uncle
Randy	50	Michael's dad
Marilyn	50	Michael's mom
George	40	Randy's friend
Guy	50	Randy's friend
Bill	40	Randy's friend

"Filmmaking should be fun, and the only way to assure that is that everything you can possibly prepare is prepared. Then you have time for the stuff that you can't prepare. If it's a bad weather day, or you lose a location, or you realize after rehearsal that the scene doesn't work, you're not completely thrown."
Jodie Foster

There will be a *list of sets* that are mentioned or described in the script.

SMOKE Set Breakdown
Exterior street outside hospital
Ice fishing lake
Exterior Michael's house – Backyard
Exterior Marilyn's car   –'74 Tan Chrysler
Exterior Michael's truck – broken-down
Interior Michael's house – Kitchen
Interior Michael's house – Parents' bedroom

There will be a *list of what the actors hold (props)* and a *list of items that will be used to decorate the sets for each location (set decoration)*.

SMOKE Props Breakdown
Michael's House
Salmon
Hunting knife
Hand-rolled cigarette
Empty bottles
Bowl of water
Body sponge
Oral syringe
Wood chips
Wheelchair

SMOKE Set Decorating Breakdown
Michael's House–Exterior
Cleaned and un-cleaned salmon
Camping cooler
Empty bottles
Package of tobacco, rolling papers
Oil drum

Pre-Production

The breakdown process continues for each of the scenes and for each of the categories. Breakdowns take time to create because each line of each scene must be analyzed in order to extract critical planning information. Regardless of how long it takes, it is a step that cannot be avoided.

In the classroom, the breakdown process is a great way to analyze the Shot List or Shooting Script that is created and translate it into an action list of what exactly is required and what exactly needs to be done.

As an example, let us return to the student film, *Water*. Once they have researched their subject and identified what they want to shoot in their script or Shot List, it is now time to break it down and begin planning.

Perhaps their Shot List looks like this:

Shot List ■ ■ ■

Shot	Video	Audio
1	Establishing wide shot of city	This is my city. This is where I live.
2	Shots of people walking down the street downtown	There are a hundred thousand people that live here. And they go through a lot of water.
3	Someone drinking from water fountain downtown	
4	Water sprinkler on lawn	
5	Car wash with water	
6	Washing dishes in a sink	
7	Swimming pool	
8	Water treatment building	And all this water comes from here!
9	Interview with water treatment plant supervisor	Supervisor talks about how much water is processed each day and why it is important to conserve water.
10	Shots inside water treatment plant of equipment working	Interview continues.

Based on the above Shot List, let's look at how students might approach breaking it down.

The first question we might ask is, "Where are we going to shoot?" The Set / Location Breakdown Form is a tool you can use to answer this question.

First let's look at the city locations mentioned—a wide shot of the city, people walking down the street, a water fountain on a street, a car wash and the water treatment plant. Let's see them in breakdown format.

Set/Location Breakdown ■ ■ ■	
Video Title: WATER	
Name of Set	**Location to be Used**
Establishing wide shot of the city	
People walking down the street	
A water fountain on a street	
A car wash	
A residential lawn	
A swimming pool	
Inside someone's kitchen	
Water treatment building	
Outside the building	
Inside the building	

This is the organizational process of breakdowns. We make a list of what we need, so that we can then find each of those requirements. As the locations are being investigated, the other departments are at work breaking down their own requirements in the same manner, scene-by-scene, and line-by-line.

Step 3. Selecting Locations

Now that we know what sets we need to find, we can start thinking about where we will actually locate them. Let's ask some questions and do some brainstorming to start the creative juices flowing and generate ideas.

Establishing wide shot of city:

- Where will you shoot this shot?
- Is there a lookout point that has a good view of the city?
- Research postcards from your community to get ideas of vantage points.
- Research where professional photographers have chosen to shoot from in the past.
- Ask around.

Suppose we know a spot from where we think we can film, perhaps called Munson's Mountain. Let's write that down. Perhaps someone suggests that it could also be filmed from Clark Mountain. Write that down too.

Set/Location Breakdown ■ ■ ■

Video Title: **WATER**

Name of Set	Location to be Used
Establishing wide shot of the city	Munson's Mtn. or Clark Mtn.
...	

Now move on to the next set. One by one, identify where each filming could take place. These may not end up being the final choices, but this is all right; it's part of the process of filmmaking. This is the process of analyzing various possibilities and making a decision as to what we think would be the best choice based on the criteria of the project.

For example, both mountains may offer spectacular views, but perhaps one is minutes from the school, and the other is a half-hour drive away. Given the time criteria of the project, which location might be more suitable for this particular project and (time) budget?

Filmmaking is an ongoing interesting exercise in problem

solving because it is a constant evaluation of balancing aesthetic and logistical choices. It is not uncommon for directors and producers to argue passionately for their idea of what the best choice might be. This applies to locations, actors, music, script, props and in short, everything.

If we look at some of the other locations, we notice that there is a requirement for a water fountain, people walking on the street, and a car wash and that these are all sets that take place downtown. I would ask the question, "Can we find a place downtown that has a water fountain and at the same time could we shoot the scene with the people walking down the street?" Further, "Can we find a downtown car wash?" We are trying to save time by finding a place downtown that can satisfy the requirements of those three shots.

Filmmakers look for groupings of similar sets and endeavour to film them at the same time, the same day or the same place. They do this because if they can reduce the time to drive around, it will increase the time they have to actually make the film.

Students' reward for distinguishing groupings and identifying patterns during the planning process is an increase of time available for the fun stuff.

Location Scouting

While we are talking about locations, let's explore the process of location scouting. Now that we know what kinds of sets we require, and we have some ideas of where those locations exist, we explore those locations by a process called 'location scouting.' In the film industry, location scouts are given written or visual descriptions of the ideal location that is desired for the scene and then they set off to find it.

They may contact a film liaison office. These offices exist in most states and provinces (and other countries) to persuade filmmakers to use the beauty and resources of the locations in their

Pre-Production

"As far as the physical pressure, this film was a big, logistical, year-in-preparation, thorough immersion for everyone who worked on it. For me, the making of this movie came down to one question: how do you eat an 8,000-pound elephant? Well, the only answer is one bite at a time. If I could give people or young filmmakers one piece of solid advice, it would be this: you don't have to make the whole movie today. You still have to make it one shot at a time. So, you have to concentrate on that one shot. The next shot can wait until you get this one done. Sometimes, the enormity of a film, or any project, becomes daunting, and anxiety and paranoia and feelings of failure can creep in. But to complete the job and do it right, you have to shoot one scene at a time."
Joel Schumacher

locale. Location scouts also investigate potential sites over the Internet, by asking other location scouts, by asking people on the street, and also by looking at their own records of locations they have utilized in the past.

The location scout presents the result of the search to the producer, director, art director and production manager. The presentation is usually in the form of assembled photographs of each of the locations, along with notes and recommendations that they have made. Once a decision has been reached as to what locations to use, the production company will arrange for the department heads to collectively visit the proposed location and evaluate firsthand the opportunities or obstacles inherent in the location. This group foray is known as a 'location survey.'

Location Survey

Filmmakers use location surveys prior to production in order to analyze and anticipate what they will find 'on the day.' Obstacles and opportunities are discussed, and solutions or plans of attack are recorded and then communicated through the department heads to the rest of the crew.

When time permits, I encourage teachers to incorporate location surveys into the process. It is a great exercise for students because it asks them to visualize, while standing at the location, what will be taking place in the future; to analyze what is required; and then to prepare sufficiently to make it all come together.

The Location Survey Form is a great starting point to examine what is required and evaluate each location's strengths and deficiencies. On the next page is a sample of a Location Survey Form.

Location Survey

■ ■ ■

Set Name: _____

Location: _____

Contact Person #1: _____

Phone #: _____

Phone #: _____

Contact Person #2: _____

Phone #: _____

Phone #: _____

Location Lighting:

What kind of natural light exists?

Skylights_____ Windows_____

Doors_____ Candlelight_____

Mirrors_____

What kind of artificial lights:

Fluorescent ____Tungsten _____

Halogen____

Is power available at location? _____

Outlets: 2 prong: ____ 3 prong__

Is there enough light,
or do you need more?

Lighting Notes:

Directions:

Parking:

Hours Available:_____

Restrooms: _____

Phone Location: _____

Equipment Access:

_____

Location Camera

Is there room to work?

To move the camera?

Where will the camera be pointing?

Camera notes:

Location Sound:

Is it quiet or noisy?

Is there traffic? Music? Machinery?

Sound Notes:

Use back of form for directions,
maps and floorplans.

Pre–Production

The Location Survey Explained

Set Name

...refers to how the script describes where the scene takes place.

Location

...is the actual address.

Contact Information

Despite planning, it is amazing how often crews arrive at a location and cannot get access because of poor communication or because the contact person forgot. (I have seen this on big budget and no budget films alike). For this reason, I like to note as much contact information as I can, and wherever possible, a backup contact person just in case.

Lighting

Before students arrive with their crew and equipment, they will want to assess the lighting requirements associated with each location.

- Is it dark?
- Do we have to bring in more lighting?
- Is it too bright?
- Do we have to pull down shades, blinds, and covers?
- Is there natural light from skylights, windows, doors, candlelight or mirrors that we could use?
- Are there artificial lights like overhead fluorescents, or tungsten, or halogen lights? (Each of these has a different colour temperature causing some to look green, orange or blue depending on how you have white balanced your camera. Any chance for exploring the colour temperature of light and other fun physics here?)
- If you are bringing additional lights, is there somewhere to plug in?

- Will the circuits take the light? Most circuits are 1500 amps and can run a couple of 750 amp lights. But if you are using two 1000 amp lights, you will need to run to two separate circuits. (Oh, the possibilities for integrating mathematics into all of this!) When in doubt, check with an expert.
- And if you are planning to plug in, what kind of electrical outlets are in the building? Are they grounded? Many old buildings only have receptacles for two-prong plugs.
- Will you need an adaptor?
- Will you need an extension cord or two?
- If you are shooting the outside of a building, does the sun shine on it all day, or is it often in shadow?
- When do you think is the best time to shoot at this location?
- Is the building or object that you are shooting reflected in a nearby building's window, or in a pool of water? Look around for creative lighting sources and creative angles.

Sound

Sound is another major consideration when choosing a location. Some locations are great visually but are too close to traffic, making it difficult or impossible to record a conversation. This is fine if you don't need to hear the sound track, or if the sound can be put in later, but usually you want to have it quiet enough to be able to record good clean sound. I have been on many location scoutings where we arrive at a possible location, close our eyes, listen, and try to hear every little thing.

- Are there airplanes above?
- Is there automobile traffic outside?
- Is there music playing?
- Is there a piece of equipment working?
- Is there construction nearby?
- Is there a barking dog?

I love this exercise because students utilize their listening skills to determine what possible audible obstacles might prevent them from a successful day of shooting, and then must decide whether to manage those sounds or to search elsewhere.

Camera

Where will the camera be? Will it be stationary or moving? How will it move? The location survey enables the camera operator, director and other key personnel to ask these questions while standing at the potential location. It is not uncommon to bring along a video camera and rough out a shot in order to look at it again back at the production office (or school).

Now you may be saying to yourself, this seems like a lot of work. Why not just shoot the scene that you need to shoot and move on? It's true, there is a lot of preparation in filmmaking, which does appear to be more work. But on a professional production, the location survey team consists of a fraction of the total film crew. It is quicker for ten people to investigate a location than a hundred. It also reduces time, money and resources wasted if those hundred people arrived at the location ready to film, but obstacles delayed them.

For student productions, depending on the grade level, the scope of the project, and the time that is available, location surveys may not be feasible. Again, my goal is to share some of the tools that filmmakers use to prepare for filming, and then let you revise, delete and incorporate as you wish. But for classrooms or schools sharing a single camera and production equipment, location scouting is a suggestion of how to stretch equipment resources further, and to ensure that the students' time with the equipment is as productive for them as possible.

Also on the sheet is room for making notes on:

Directions	• How do we get from the school to there?
Parking	• Where do we park cars or the school bus?
Hours available	• When would we have access to the location?
Restrooms	• Where are the closest restrooms?

Communication	• Is there a phone at this location that we can use?
Notes	• What other information should we record?

Use the back page to make maps and floor plans of the buildings or locations being surveyed.

Step 4. What Equipment Do We Need?

Once we know where we are shooting, and sometimes even before, we have to start thinking about what kind of equipment we will require. For our film, *Smoke*, the questions were about which cameras we would be using, what kind of dollies, cranes and other camera moving tools that we would require.

In the classroom, an investigation of the equipment required must also occur. There may only be one camera in the classroom or in the school, so the kind of camera may not be as important a question as whether we can we get it? This is a scheduling question and we'll look at that soon. We can still identify what kind of camera, sound, lighting and other equipment will be required.

We can look at how we are going to film each scene and ask about what kinds of camera moving equipment we might want to illustrate our ideas. Schools may not be equipped with expensive motion picture cranes and dollies, but by being resourceful, students can still achieve the effect that camera cranes and dollies bring to the look of the film. As we said earlier, filmmaking is about problem solving and resourcefulness.

I was once working as a producer on a feature film with a moderate budget of about four million dollars. The director, Mort Ransen, who made the award-winning film *Margaret's Museum*, loved the location that we had found for his latest story. We went on a location survey prior to production and he brought the actions from the script to life, as he explained each shot.

One idea was to have an actor emerge out of a barn, and run

around in large circles until he collapsed, exhausted, on the ground under the night sky. He showed us where he wanted the camera to be in the middle of that circle and how he wanted it to turn around quickly while watching the actor run.

As part of the producing team, we met with the head of the camera department and the grip department and explored how we were going to shoot this. We could not shoot it from the tripod, and we could not dolly around fast enough. There was a special crane we could rent that would allow the camera to hang in the centre of the set, turn around quickly, and get the shot the director envisioned.

Upon some research it was discovered that the cost of the rental, the travel time to deliver it to where we were filming (a day away), the operator fees, and the weather contingency brought the cost of this shot to around $15,000. This shot was not planned for in the script and it certainly was not in the budget. We tried to find less expensive equipment but they did not produce the shot that the director wanted.

One day at a production meeting, as we were going through all the remaining obstacles on the production, John Kuchera, the key grip, stood up and said, "The accountant's chair!" We all looked at him like he was crazy and then realized that he was talking about how we might get this circling shot. We all marched to the accountant's office, ordered him off his swivelling chair and took it to the middle of the studio. The cameraman was given a little DV video camera and the director ran around the studio as John turned the accountant's chair around in fast circles to follow him.

"Faster!" yelled the cameraman. "Too fast!" he yelled. "Perfect!"

So a week later, when it came to filming the scene, we had the accountant's chair in the middle of the field, with a piece of plywood attached to the seat so that two people could sit on it (one to operate the camera and one to focus the lens), and we solved the $15,000 obstacle with a piece of plywood, gaffer tape, an accountant's chair and a little imagination.

The filmmaking process is not about technology. It is about problem solving, resourcefulness, experimentation, teamwork, creativity, and the self-esteem and pride that result from overcoming the impossible. This is why obstacles in the classroom filmmaking process are so wonderful, because they are such rich opportunities to challenge minds and provide the excitement of real world problem-solving experiences.

I have seen students use wheelchairs, skateboards, wheelbarrows, roller skates and accounting chairs to achieve fluid camera movement. I have seen teeter totters as cranes, and ladders and scaffold turned into camera platforms. The important thing is for them to dream what they want to do. The details will follow.

Step 5. Refining the Team

Another question to ask is: who is going to make this happen? Which individuals are required, exactly, to make this project come to life?

There may be the student group itself. This group may consist of the producer, director, camera people, interviewer, etc. But who else will be required to make all this happen?

- Who will drive the crew to these locations?
- Who are the contacts at the location?
- What other experts are involved?
- Who are we borrowing equipment from?
- Who do we talk to if the camera breaks down?
- Who are all the people involved directly and indirectly in our project, and how do we keep track and communicate with each other?

Filmmakers often use a document that is simply and appropriately called the Contact List. I find this an extremely useful information sheet that I refer to constantly during all phases

Contact List ▪ ▪ ▪

Date: ___Sept 15___   Page __1__ of __1__

___Water___   Mr. Theosdosakis

Project Title   Executive Producer

Position	Name and Address	Telephone /Email
Executive Producer	Mr. Theodosakis	nikos@email.com 496-5348
Director Camera Sound	Mary S.	496-5455
Editor	Sophie D.	496-9001
Producer	Chris D.	490-1234 chris@clearwater.com
Water Treatment Plant Supervisor	Mr. Pante 23 Aqua Road	490-0000 pante@clearwater.com
Water Treatment Plant Administrator	Crystal Clearwater	490-1122

of the filmmaking process. It lists the crew, cast and other contacts, their titles and functions, and how to contact them (email, phone, address, etc.).

On a feature film, the Contact List is sometimes divided into three documents, one each for cast, crew and other contacts. I encourage its use in the classroom because it demonstrates what a team-based activity filmmaking is. The preparation and use of the Contact List clarifies to both the student and the teacher:

- Who is involved?
- In what capacity?
- And of course, how can they be contacted?

I have spoken to several teachers who now incorporate this kind of document as one of the filmmaking steps, and insist on a copy before they allow cameras and equipment to be signed out.

Step 6. Scheduling

Scheduling is another important part of the filmmaking process. Typically, the producer, production manager, assistant director and the director get together and ask the question: When will this be shot, exactly? And in what order?

Because big budget filmmaking is about bringing together dozens or hundreds of skilled technicians and hundreds of thousands of dollars in equipment, the time that is required of those resources is very expensive. The order of filming is often non-sequential so that time can be saved. Saved time translates into saved money. Saved money translates into resources that can be re-allocated into other areas to help make the film the best it can be.

The production team has to decide in what order the scenes should be shot and when exactly they need to schedule actors, crew and all the other equipment and resources. Sometimes it is not only about what day, but sometimes what hour of that day, even if that day is a month or months in the future.

"I think that why so many of the older directors were good was because they had a discipline that was imposed from outside. I think there is nothing better than being told, "Look, you've got to do it in three days; you've only got this much money, and do it, kid, or you're not going to get it done." You should have that kind of pressure making movies or anything else, that sense of economy."
Peter Bogdanovich

Add to this the inevitable time conflicts that arise from actor and crew schedules from other films, equipment and location availability, travel constraints, weather surprises, labour regulations, human error and script changes. As you can imagine, scheduling a feature film is an exercise in patience, vision, problem solving and experimentation. It is truly an art unto itself.

Traditionally, filmmakers use a tool called the Production Board to help schedule the production and to keep track of all the information. It is an 18" x 48" board that can hold dozens of thin strips of cardboard. The planning department, primarily the assistant director, looks at the strips and arranges them in groups based on similar locations or similar actors. The strips are arranged from left to right in the order that they will be filmed. At the end of each day's grouping of shots, a cardboard strip that marks the end of that day is placed in the sequence. And so it continues until all the strips are accounted for. The advantage of this kind of paper system is that it requires no batteries, is extremely portable, and can be updated on location by rearranging one or more of the strips.

Although students might want to experiment with this kind of information-sorting tool, I personally would like to see them create their own electronic databases as an opportunity to develop yet another skill in the filmmaking process.

Students can decide what fields of information are necessary to consider, and create a new record for each scene. There could be information on who is in it, where it is being filmed, how long they think it will take, and anything else that they think valuable. Once they are finished, the records can be sorted by location, actors, or any other criteria, and arranged in order for filming.

On a more ambitious level, databases in film production scheduling can include 360-degree panoramic photographs of where the location will take place, movie files of actors, infinite details of what is required and where it is coming from, and of course any other field that might facilitate communication and planning.

Most schools have neither an abundance of video cameras and equipment, nor an abundance of teacher and student hours available for assistance, so scheduling is not only helpful, but in some cases crucial for the successful realization of the production.

For students, scheduling is more than just deciding what happens when. It can be a great experience in estimating, research, creative problem solving, and also in the satisfaction of making the giant jigsaw puzzle all work. It is an experience that benefits the students with lifelong scheduling skills.

Shooting Schedule

The question, "When does it happen?" is answered with a document called the Shooting Schedule. All the results of analyzing the detailed scheduling requirements are communicated to the filmmaking team through this tool.

Here is the Shooting Schedule for *Smoke*:

Shooting Schedule

Date: Nov 15
Video Title: SMOKE : Day 1 - Nov 15

Scene#	Scene Description	Pages	Characters
1	Ext. Hospital - Day Michael rides up and Tyler and Jordan tease him	6/8 pgs	1,.5.6
2	Ext. Michael's Backyard Michael watches Ron clean fish	6/8	1,3
4	Ext. Michael's Backyard Ron tells Michael about his father	3/8	1,3
...			

The number in the first column is the scene number that was allocated when the Script became the Shooting Script.

The second column describes the set where it takes place and a brief description of the action that occurs.

The third column lists what fraction of a page this scene represents. A scene which covers one full script page would be represented with a '1.' Pages are divided into eighths. A scene that lasts 1/2 a page is shown as '4/8,' a scene that is 3/4 of a page long is recorded as '6/8.' This gives the cast and crew a quick reminder of how long the scene is and how long it might take to shoot. On a professional feature film, a typical day might be to try and film three or four pages. So if the director and assistant director try to shoot four pages a day, the fractions of each scene should not add up to more than the number four on any one day. (Can you see the great math tie-in here?)

The numbers in the final column correspond to cast numbers from the cast breakdown sheet. This lets the filmmaking team know at a glance which characters are required each day.

Why would a class take the time to create a Shooting Schedule? Let me offer two reasons:
- to avoid wasted time during production
- to stretch limited resources (equipment and people) over multiple projects

For example, let's look at the water conservation project we mentioned earlier. The Shooting Schedule that each group creates articulates their intent of what they plan to shoot, and the order in which they plan to shoot it.

Perhaps each group is allowed six hours of camera time over two days, so as to allow other groups (or other classes) to also gain access to the camera. In this example, the group organizes their Shooting Schedule by locations. Sometimes film schedules are organized by actor availability, weather forecasts, expensive equipment rental, budget limitations and other factors. But usually, they are sorted by location because the fewer number of times you have to move people to the same location, the more time (money) is saved.

For the science film, *Water*, a scheduling breakdown might look like the sample on the following page. I have replaced the page count column used on film sets with a simpler estimating method. The time

"I have found one of the hardest lessons to learn, particularly in preproduction, is how to budget your time. Now this might sound entirely insensitive. It isn't. Because most of the solutions you arrive at in preproduction are going to solve an enormous number of production problems."
Franklin Schaffner

Shooting Schedule ■ ■ ▢

Date: **September 15**

Video Title: **WATER**

Day 1 - September 23

Scene#	Scene Description	Time Required
1	Ext. Munson's Mountain - Day Establishing shot of the City	One hour
8	Ext. Water Treatment Plant – Day Establishing shot of the plant and sign	1/2 hour
9	Int. Water Treatment Plant-Day Interview with plant manager	One hour
10	Int. Water Treatment Plant - Day Cutaway shots of water treatment plant	1/2 hour

Day 2 - September 24

Scene#	Scene Description	Time Required
2	Ext. Downtown – Day Crowd walks down street	1/2 hour
3	Ext. Downtown – Day Child drinks from water fountain	15 minutes
5	Ext. Downtown – Day Car Wash	1/2 hour
4	Ext. Front Yard – Day Water sprinkler on lawn	One hour
7	Ext. Backyard – Day Swimming pool	15 minutes
6	Int. Kitchen – Day Washing dishes in a sink	1/2 hour

Pre-Production

in the far right column represents how long the students estimate the footage will take to be recorded. This estimate includes the time that it takes to set up and wrap (the disassembling of equipment and sets that is required in order to leave the location).

As in the above examples, the development of schedules requires the estimation of how much time is required for each shot or scene to be recorded.

On a professional production, the decisions made in scheduling affect the budget. The two are linked closely to each other. Schedules and budgets. If you fall behind schedule, you will surely go over budget. If you are ahead of schedule, you'll probably go over budget anyway (kidding).

Contingency Planning

When filmmakers plan to make their movies, they also plan that sometimes things go wrong, so a big part of scheduling is integrating a backup plan for every day that is scheduled. On every schedule on every film, there is a little note that the assistant director makes about their contingency plan.

One of the most common things to sour a planned day is rain. So when the production department plans the scenes for any day of filming, they almost always note a 'cover set' which announces what will be filmed under cover in the event that it rains. It's a 'just in case' thing.

Imagine a film crew arriving at 6:00 a.m. to a park where scenes are to be filmed, only to find it is raining. They cannot afford to have all the actors and technicians wait while the producer or production team decides what to do or where to go. These decisions are made ahead of time, in anticipation of rain or of other things going wrong.

It's an interesting concept and one that I think warrants discussion with students. If nothing else, I find it interesting how filmmakers anticipate obstacles and failure into the filmmaking process. They analyze these potential tragedies and strategize how they will conquer them.

For students, try this exercise once all the planning is done. Have them write down ten things that might go wrong that would prevent them from getting the scene. Now, what can they do to prevent that from happening?

"The director is simply the audience. . . . His job is to preside over accidents."
Orson Welles

Step 7. *Budgeting*

Budgets. The mere mention of the word sends shivers down my spine. Alas, filmmaking is an expensive process, so we endure the details and rigor that are contained in those ten-to sixty-page documents so that films can be made.

Just as the Script is a blueprint for the story, the Budget is a blueprint for spending. It is usually about the spending of money, but it has potential in the classroom to be much more. Time is one of the unreplenishable resources that we have in filmmaking, both in big budget movies and in classroom projects.

If you are up for the challenge, or if you want your students to exercise their mathematical skills (or if you want to combine learning outcomes based on mathematics), you may consider adding budgeting as part of your filmmaking project. This tends to work better with middle school ages and higher, but hey, surprise me! The producer of each group is usually assigned the responsibility of presenting it to the teacher, but it can be filled in or calculated by the entire group.

The Budget looks at the pre-production, production and post-production phases of filmmaking and asks what is being done and how long it will take.

In the following sample, the column 'Budget' refers to how many group hours are being allocated to the task and to the phase. This may include in-school and after-school time, or school only, or any combination you feel appropriate.

For added difficulty, have students create a spreadsheet, tracking individual hours for each task. For more fun, assign an hourly dollar amount to each student's work and have part of the assignment to create a spreadsheet with dollar amounts and variables. For example, each individual's hourly rate could be $100.00, while camera use is $500.00 a day. Editing equipment could be by the day or by the hour. Perhaps they have a budget of $10,000 to create this film.

Budget

■ ■ ■

Project Title: ___WATER___

Date: ___Sept 15___   Executive Producer: ___Mr. Theodosakis___

Development/ Pre-production	When	Budget	Total Hours	
➤ Script	September 16	2 hrs		
➤	September 17	2 hrs	4 hrs	
➤ Storyboard	September 18	2 hrs	2 hrs	
➤				
➤ Planning	September 19	4 hrs	4 hrs	
	TOTAL:			10

Production	When	Budget	Total Hours	
Scene #				
1. View of City	September 23 10am – 1pm	1 hr 30min		
8. Ext. Water Treatment Building		1 hr 30min		
9. Interview			3 hr	
10. Interior Water Treatment		30min		
	September 25 10am – 1 pm			
2. People walking down street		15min		
3. Water Fountain		30min		
5. Car wash		1 hr		
4. Sprinkler		15min		
7. Swimming Pool		30min		
6. Dishes (interior kitchen)			3 hr	
	TOTAL:			6

Post-Production	When	Budget	Total Hours	
Logging	September 25 1:30 – 3 pm	1.5 hrs	1.5 hr	
Paper Edit	September 26 9am – 3 pm	3 hrs		
Assembly		4 hrs	7 hrs	
Picture Editing	September 27 9am – 3pm	3 hrs		
Sound Editing		3 hrs	6 hrs	
Titles and Finishing	Sept 30 10am-2pm	3 hr		
Export		1 hr	4 hrs	
Test Screening	Sept 31 10am	1 hr	1 hr	
Revisions	Sept 31 2pm	2 hr	2 hr	
	TOTAL:			21.5

Do you see any potential for incorporating mathematical and technological skill development outcomes in this science film?

As with scheduling, it is always an eye opener to see how long things actually take to shoot. Later, during production, we will use Call Sheets and Production Reports to see how the estimation of time requirements compared with what actually happened.

Step 8.   *Problem Solving*

Following the creation of the budget and the schedule (and usually the budget does come first, but we are adapting here), there comes a time to do a little problem solving. The expectations that the schedule demands and the resources that the budget affords often do not match.

Filmmakers need to identify and solve problems arising from budgeting or scheduling deficiencies and conflicts; they do this with creative problem solving. When you do not have enough time or money to solve the problem, what do you do?

- You can find more resources.
- You can delete the scene.
- You can find a way to keep the scene, still make it great, and use fewer resources all at the same time.

For example, Linda and I once produced a comedy called *The Date*. One of the scenes had the father (Jay Brazeau) catching a fly and taking it outside to the porch to feed to his spider. We looked at ideas on how we were going to shoot this scene, and we talked to a special effects friend who gave us some ideas ranging from mechanical spiders to matte paintings.

All of the ideas were too expensive for our small budget and we were disappointed. I wanted to cut the scene. Linda, who wrote it, maintained that it had to stay. The problem was that our budget did not allow for the effect to be included. We did not want to use a silly little plastic spider or anything to degrade the overall production quality of the film, but we did not know what we could do.

In discussing the scene with our friend, cinematographer Harvey LaRocque, he suggested that we not see the spider at all. He suggested instead that the scene could be shot from the spider's POV (Point of View). Our director of photography Charles LaVack took it further and experimented with lighting and lenses and how to make it all work with shadows and implied spiders.

In the end, the scene was shot from a high angle, simulating the spider's POV looking down at the father and his daughter's date (Scott Anderson) as they stand there watching the fly about to be eaten. With a few sound effects and this innovative solution, we avoided using special effects, and came up with a fun way to tell the story of that scene. Interestingly, we got to that innovative place because we were pushed into a corner by our high expectations and our tiny budget.

I promise you this: if you invite filmmaking into your teaching, you will hear success stories of how your students overcame obstacles to achieve their movies. And those stories are often accompanied by broad grins and beaming eyes! Imagine what hurdles are waiting to be overcome!

Step 9. *Communicating to the Team*

Another important part of the final preparation is communicating to the team what has been decided in this planning stage. What this means is sending those breakdowns, schedules, budgets, contact lists, and everything else that lists the details of the production to everyone on the crew.

Information is power. If your crew does not have the information when they need it, or if they do not have updated information (as things change), mistakes will happen. Trust me, I know.

Don't be stuck on using the forms I have provided. I would love to see students develop their own forms, and in fact, I envision them moving from these paper/digital forms to web-based production forms that they can share and update with team members. I am working on some now, and they will be available at <*www.directorintheclassroom.com*> when the tinkering is done.

Eventually we will see the day (I don't think too far away), when student filmmakers will have all their planning documents on their hand-held computers and will be notified of changes every time they switch them on. Real time budgeting and scheduling will take place, and communicating with others will be both unobtrusive and precise.

Step 10. Final Preparations

The schedules are created, the budgets are created, the checklists are complete, the equipment is booked, and the locations are confirmed. "Can we please start now?" Soon. Just a few quick notes on final preparation first.

Rehearsal

If you have actors involved, it is a good idea for the director to rehearse the actors prior to the day of shooting. This enables the director and actors to explore how they are going to approach the performance without the pressure of everyone else on the crew watching or waiting. As well, preparation during the planning stage will save time during the production phase.

If you or your students are interested in the rehearsal process, or in understanding how directors and actors prepare for filming, I would recommend the book I mentioned earlier called *Directing Actors*, by Judith Weston. It is simply the best book in the galaxy about how directors and actors work together. It speaks about the rehearsal process in detail as well as offering extensive insight on preparation and production from a performance perspective. I wish I had read it when I first started out, but unfortunately she hadn't written it yet. (Lucky you, it's out there now!)

Pre-Production

Ideas Change

Congratulations! You have survived a long chapter. Ah, but now can you see why I am so excited by planning and filmmaking in the classroom.

Filmmaking is planning. It is about details, schedules and budgets. It incorporates mathematics, communication, physics, language arts, problem solving and research. It entails disappointments, surprises and adventure.

It's all this and more.

As students work their way through the planning process, and as they research and assemble the details that will build their film, they will inevitably make discoveries. These are the subtle, sometimes drastic changes that continue to shape and shade their films.

Ideas change.

As long as there is an awareness of what the planning processes are, there is great potential for students to take what they have learned through filmmaking and transfer it to other areas throughout their lives. These include other projects that they will plan such as investigating a new job, buying a house, learning a new skill, starting their own business, or preparing to take a trip outside their community.

Once again, filmmaking is about learning real world skills that can be used forever. Okay, let's shoot a film.

14: Production

Now the fun begins; we're ready to unpack the cameras, load up the tape, and start recording images and sounds.

Did you notice that during the previous six steps of the filmmaking process, defining, developing the idea, pitching, screenwriting, storyboarding, and planning that we have not been dependent on technology?

The processes involved with imagining, planning and preparation incorporate skills of problem solving, analysis, visualization, investigation and communication. The process is not about software or hardware, but about mind ware.

Now we pick up our cameras, lights and microphones, and record the footage that is required to fulfill our vision and construct our films. I am not going to go into the details of how to operate a camera, how to light a set, or how to record audio. Those specific techniques are outside the scope of this book, and it is a topic that is covered very well in many books as well as in the equipment's instruction manual. Rather than providing technical information, I prefer to look at the production stage in terms of the processes, planning and student benefits involved. So here we go.

Developing Problem Solving and Logic Skills

When the first day of filming arrives, it is time for a few more documents to be in place. These documents can be part of the planning process, but it was such a big chapter, I thought I would give you a break.

- The Production Checklist
- The Shot List
- The Call Sheet
- The Production Report

Actually, Call Sheets and Shot Lists may be sketched out during planning, but they are revised or created in detail on a daily basis during the entire phase of production. No matter what size of production, and no matter how much time was spent planning, something always comes up that was not expected. Because of this, these documents are revised in accordance with what is really required, as opposed to what was thought to be required.

The Production Checklist

This is a checklist to make sure that all the equipment and supplies that we have planned for are at hand—fully charged batteries, tripod, blank tapes, a few quarters for phone calls, etc. The sample Production Checklist on the following page lists some basic requirements, but it will change for each production. After each project is recorded, I encourage students to consider what other equipment or supplies they would have preferred to have on their checklist, and then add it immediately for the next group's project. Other classrooms can also be involved, and a sharing of information encouraged to keep enhancing the equipment list.

You may want to have two columns on the right-hand side as shown below. This way you can easily record what went out of the classroom studio (or when) and what was returned.

Production Checklist	Out	In
CAMERA		
Camera		
Tripod		
Blank tapes (extras as well)		
Batteries (extras as well)		
AC power supply for camera		
LIGHTING		
Light kit		
Power cables		
Clamps/clothes pins		
Stands		
Gel stock (colour correction)		
AUDIO		
Microphones (wired or wireless or both as backup)		
Microphone cables		
Headphones		
Boom pole		
MISC		
Duct tape (gaffer tape if you have the budget)		
Pen/paper (for field notes)		
Personal Release Forms		
Video monitor (to check signal)		
Scripts		
Shot List		
Storyboard		

Production

Reviewing the Shot List

When we arrive on location we have the Shot List, Script and Storyboard documents as guides to what we want to film.

The Shot List contributes in the following ways:

- It informs us of the subject of each shot.
- It informs us of the kind of shots (close-up, establishing) that are required.
- It helps to determine the order in which the shots could be recorded.

The Shot List may be a simple outline of what is required from each set, or it may be a detailed document of what exact angles, movement, and lens choices the director has pre-selected.

Shot Lists melt into Storyboards, which have sometimes melted out of Scripts. The three are all different but related as they all identify what has to be shot to tell the story. They each contribute something. The Script provides the details, the Storyboard provides visual notes, and the Shot List provides an organizational strategy. I encourage the use of all of them.

As in the science project on water conservation we arrive at the water treatment plant with a reminder of what shots we would like to record. The Shot List for *Water* calls for an establishing image of the water treatment plant from outside the building. It requires shots of the machines working inside, as well as the interview with the supervisor. So to help us create the movie that we are planning to make, each of these segments must be recorded.

How would you approach getting those three shots? Is there a logical order? Personally, I would make sure that our contact, in this case the supervisor, was actually there. I would want to confirm with him that he was not planning to leave. I would hate to do all my exterior filming and interior filming and then discover when I went to interview him that he had left for lunch. So, I would probably want to contact him upon my arrival, confirm his availability, and be prepared to work around his schedule.

"It's usually how I write the script—I make sure the actors give the on-camera performance that I heard in my head when I was I writing."
Kevin Smith

Reviewing the Storyboards

While filming, it is also a good idea to review the Storyboards because they remind us about:

- Framing and composition notes
- Camera angles
- Lighting
- Camera movement
- Subject movement within the frame
- Subject direction

Reviewing the Script

The Script enables us to see the context of the shot we plan to film.

As you prepare to film a shot, it is helpful to ask yourself, "What happens before this shot?" and "What happens after this shot?" Asking these questions may help create ideas for appropriate transitions from one shot to the next. These questions are invaluable for actors who are filming dramas out of sequence. Asking where their character was before this scene happened helps them discover the emotional circumstances that exist when the present scene unfolds.

The Script reminds us what the connection is between the separate images that we record, and it helps clarify what the purpose is of each specific shot. In addition to the Script, Shot List, and Storyboards, it is extremely important that we be aware of other opportunities for shots at that location.

For example, perhaps we are at the location and we see a poster for water conservation on the building wall. We should shoot that poster just in case we can use it, or in case we need it later on in editing. This gets back to the idea of letting the location surprise you and allowing it to help shape ideas for enhancing the film.

The production stage of filmmaking seems to bounce between the boundaries that have been set out in the Script, Shot List and

Call Sheet ■ ■ □

Production:	**Smoke**	Shooting Day:	1
Producer:	Theodosakis	Date:	15-Sep
Director:	Theodosakis	Crew Call:	8:00AM
Ass. Director	Davidson	Weather:	Sun with cloudy periods

SET	SCENES	PAGES	CAST NOS.	LOCATION
1 Ext. Hospital	1,	"4/8	1,5,6	1)Healthcare Building
2 Ext. Michaels Backyard	2,	"3/8	1,3	687 Main Street,
2 Ext. Michaels Backyard	4,	"4/8	1.3	Penticton
				2) Thompson House
				2106 Naramata Road
				Naramata

NO.	CAST MEMBER	PART OF	MAKE-UP	SET CALL	REMARKS
1	Kevin W.	Michael	7:00am	8:00am	
3	Ken S.	Uncle Ron	12pm	1:00am	Don't Shave
5	Louis B.G.	Tyler	7:00am	8:00am	
6	Thomas S.	Billy	7:00am	8:00am	

ATMOSPHERE & STANDINS	PROPS	SPECIAL INSTRUCTIONS
none	Bicycles (3)	Fire & Smoke for Backyard Set
	Cooler	2 Fire Extinguishers On Set
	Fish	
	Knife	

OTHER CALL TIMES:				VEHICLES & OTHER:	
Director	7	Camera	8	Uncle Ron's Truck	
First A.D.	7	Sound	8	Father's Truck (On blocks)	
Second A.D.	7	Grips	8	Mother's Car	
Prod. Asst.	7	Electric	8		
Craft Services	7	Art Dept.	8		
Script Supr.	7	Make-up	7		
Dir. of Photo	7	Wardrobe	##		

CHANGES AND OTHER INFO:

In case of rain, we'll shoot scene 10, Michael in his home at Johny Donair Studios, 219 Main

After lunch, company move to 2106 Naramata Road (about 10 minutes drive)

Storyboard, as well as the opportunities encountered while in production.

The Call Sheet

Filmmakers use a tool called the Call Sheet to communicate information to the team about exactly what is planned and expected for a particular day of shooting. It is a sheet of paper that is distributed to all the members of the filmmaking team and it contains the most up-to-date schedule and scene information.

The assistant director and his department sometimes produce it during the planning process but it is only 'published' officially the day or night before the filming occurs.

I like to have students produce Call Sheets not only so they can improve their chances for a successful shoot, but also so they can have more experience with the planning and thinking processes involved.

Some of the most frustrating comments I hear from students and teachers are about how time is wasted and how confusion dampens the spirit of the production. Most often, both are the result of a lack of communication. Basic information like knowing exactly where everyone is supposed to meet and at exactly what time can be easily overlooked. I have heard many students tell me that they went somewhere only to find they were in the wrong place or that someone changed it but no one told them. Call Sheets are intended to eliminate this kind of miscommunication.

The Call Sheet for the first day of filming *Smoke* lists:
- What scenes are planned for filming
- What actors are required
- When everyone is supposed to meet
- Where everyone is meeting
- What will happen in case it rains
- Special instructions

If students hand in a Call Sheet as one of the prerequisites

"The more you can plan in advance, the better. And the more decisions you've made before you ever get to the set, the better. But you have to stay open to the moments of discovery. You have to keep your heart open to the magic."
James Cameron

for taking out the equipment, it will assure both the teacher and student that preparation has occurred and the team is ready to shoot.

I also like using Call Sheets because they outline the steps and goals on a daily basis of what it is going to take to move towards the shared vision of the final film. It answers the question, "What do we plan to achieve on this day?"

A simplified version of the Call Sheet is available on the attached CD and may be more appropriate for student documentary-style projects like *Water*.

Regardless of what format you use, the important thing about using Call Sheets in a classroom filmmaking environment is that it aligns the team, focuses the work, and encourages good planning and communication.

Being 'In the Moment'

Sometimes when you read or hear about directors and actors talking about their work process, they refer to being 'in the moment.' It is a hard term to define but it relates to being so engaged and immersed in your work that new ideas materialize inside of you and these ideas often bring a freshness that makes the work better.

For actors it may be to instinctively alter their performance halfway though a scene in a way that creates a more compelling performance. For directors, it may be about discovering possibilities to enhance performance or visual choices.

In a word, it is about inspiration. I mention this here because the same thing can happen in the creative process of production. Students become 'inspired' and ponder the magic question, "What if?"

Being in the moment is about allowing one's self to recognize that these instances of inspiration do occur and then to have the conviction and courage to say to the others on the crew, "What if we tried this?"

"When you do not know what you are doing and what you are doing is the best—that is inspiration."
Robert Bresson

This is where you start trying things and experimenting intuitively. Again, the more you film, the more comfortable you become experimenting with those ideas that pop into your head on set. On professional productions and school projects alike, this is the great challenge to filmmakers. How close do you stick to what you planned to shoot versus how far do you allow yourself to explore new material 'in the moment'?

A suggestion may be to advise students to get what they think they need according to their research and preparation (their Shot List, Storyboard, Script) and then, according to their inspirations, record as much additional footage as they can.

When you are on a set directing you cannot help but see new opportunities for shots, angles or even entire scenes because the actors, locations and sets inspire you. Sometimes a small prop that you spot on a table can get your mind going on how to stage a scene in a new way. I find it helpful to blurt out my ideas to my assistant director. I suggest writing them down to keep track of 'dream shots' that I would love to get at some point in the day or later on during production.

The key is to experiment. Encourage wild shooting ideas and sudden brainstorms. During editing, students will start to develop a sense of what footage tends to end up in finished pieces and what does not. As a result, next time they are planning a movie, or out shooting one, they can incorporate what they have experienced and instantly analyze and decide what kind of shots they require for telling their story.

As you can see, it is a circle of learning. The more you film, the more you learn how to film. The more you learn how to film, the more you can see how much you have to learn about filming.

Production Report

If the Call Sheet answers the question, "What do we plan to do?" then the Production Report answers the question, "What

Here is the Production Report for *Smoke*, Day 1.

Production Report

		Scheduled	Revised	Actual
Day	1	1st Unit	5	0	1

		Date	15-Nov	2nd Unit	0	0	0

Production: **Smoke**

Producer:	Theodosakis	Date	15-Nov	2nd Unit	0	0	0

					Scheduled	Revised	Actual
Production: **Smoke**	Date	15-Nov	2nd Unit	0	0	0
Producer: Theodosakis	Date Started	15-Nov	Rehearsals	3		3
Director: Theodosakis	Sched Finish	19-Nov	Travel			
Ass. Director: Davidson	Status	On Schedule	Holiday			
				Total	8	0	4

Crew Call	8:00	Wrap to	20:00
Shooting Call	9:30	Last out	20:00 Camera
First Shot	10:35		19:00 Grip
Lunch	12:00 to 13:00		19:30 Electric
Last Shot	18:30		

	Minutes	Set Ups	Added		Script Scenes		Pages
Previous	0:00	0	0	Original	12		9
Today	2:30	10	0	Revised			
Total	2:30	10	0	Taken Previously	0		0
				Taken today	3		1 7/8th
				Taken to date	0		0
				To be taken	9		7 1/8th

Scenes	Set:	Location
	1 Ext. Hospital	Healthcare Building
	2 Ext. Michaels Backyard	687 Main Street, Penticton
	4 Ext. Michaels Backyard	Thompson House
		2106 Naramata Road, Naramata

Cast	Character	report to set	Dismiss	Meals
Kevin W.	1 Michaell	w	8:00	18:40 1200-1300
Ken S.	3 Uncle Ron	w	1:00	18:40
Louis B.G.	5 Tyler	w	8:00	12:00 1200-1300
Thomas S.	6 Jordan	w	8:00	12:00 1200-1300

NOTES:

Burton K lightly burnt hand   on smoker.

Scene 4 may have to be reshot, the weather became quite windy, and the trees blowing in the background may not match the background in scene 2-check footage.

actually happened?" At the end of each shooting day, on probably every film and television production in the world, a document is generated that says, "This is what happened." The Production Report is usually created by the assistant directors and submitted to the production manager and the producers. It tells a story in numbers and facts of how the day went, what goals were met, and what setbacks occurred.

The Production Report is essentially an evaluation tool, which looks at the performance of the filmmaking team against the goals set out by that same team. What I love about students using Production Reports is that it gives them an opportunity for reflection and self-evaluation while the events of the day are still fresh in their minds.

The act of recording what actually happened and comparing it to what was planned gives students instant assessment of their estimation and planning skills. If fifteen shots were planned and all fifteen were shot, wonderful, congratulations, they have a future in this business! They have demonstrated proficiency not only in organizing, planning and production but also in estimating, creating logical schedules, and fully utilizing their resources.

If not all the shots were recorded, wonderful, congratulations, learning is about to occur. It is in those deficiencies that there exists great potential for learning about planning.

The experience of not allowing enough time for recording a shot and rushing to complete it is not quickly forgotten. As students prepare to schedule their next production, they can draw upon this collection of production experiences, both great and wanting. The more projects students experience, the more they can sharpen estimation skills and schedule accordingly.

I love the spot on the Production Report for both a film like *Smoke* and a student project like *Water* which asks the question, "If something went wrong, why did it go wrong?" The Notes section is a space in which to capture that information.

I once worked on a feature film where on the first day of filming the people in charge of bringing the car (which was a big part of the movie) forgot to bring it to the set. Despite it being planned for, despite it being on the Call Sheet, this mistake happened. We lost almost two hours while they scrambled to bring it from the other side of town. We started late and we missed our last shot of the day because of it. This is exactly the kind of event that would be recorded on the Production Report, not to lay blame, but to analyze what went wrong and then create safeguards from it occurring again.

The Production Report is a tool for learning about how we work. It offers students experience in critically looking at what they learned from their productions, and articulating those experiences on paper. By taking the time to analyze what happened, students will discover how to learn from their own experiences. This is a skill that will not only make them better film producers, but will also make them better producers of ideas throughout their lives.

Ideas Change

Once again, ideas change.

The many forces of people, time and resources shade the production process. Delays, miscommunication, bad weather, dead batteries, faulty equipment, misplaced footage or simply lack of time all affect how the idea will be communicated.

Likewise, great weather, community cooperation, good fortune, good planning, good advice and on-set inspiration and brilliance affect how the story will be recorded and told. All of these circumstances of production, both frustrating and rewarding, are part of the total learning experience of filmmaking and a great illustration of why ideas change once again.

15: Editing

Filmmakers often say that movies are made in the editing room. In this chapter you'll discover why.

Editing is about taking all the audio and video materials that have been generated and collected during the production phase and assembling them into the best possible sequence that communicates a specific idea. The decisions made during the post-production phase will have as much an impact on your audience as all the decisions that have been made up to this point.

Some people refer to editing as the final draft of the screenplay because the editor has the power to re-write the story based on decisions of what to include, what to delete, what to enhance, and what to diminish.

It is possible to write one film on paper, photograph another on the set, and watch a different one on screen, all because of shifts in perspective and point of view. This is one of the reasons that directors want to be involved in the editing of their films.

Developing Higher Order Thinking Skills

The great benefit of editing for student filmmakers is that it provides opportunities to exercise tremendous amounts of critical thinking.

Editing requires the viewing and analysis of many minutes (or hours) of video footage in order to make decisions on what to include and what to leave out. This analysis is based on the relationship of the footage collected to the theme or subject of the filmmaking assignment. As well as analysis, the editing process requires students to synthesize that footage and material, and shape it into a finished form that communicates their ideas to an audience.

When students do not have the footage they require, they use creative problem solving to find out how they will find or

"This, of course, was one of the elements of the Eisenstein film that was so exciting. How the editing was able to take—that's always fascinating—take this, and this, and put it together, and have something come out that was neither of those two things. Of course, the sense of rhythm that editing can do!"
Francis Ford Coppola

Post-Production

substitute that footage. Editing incorporates research skills as they investigate footage from other students, the Web and other resources.

Editing enables students to experiment creatively in terms of how images are juxtaposed, how they cut or dissolve together, how titles are used and how music and sound are incorporated. It requires massive amounts of organizational aptitude to keep track of all the elements such as the digital video footage, the photographs, the sound recordings, and the music tracks .

Editing develops time management skills through the use of planning tools like paper edits, and through the scheduling and sharing of the editing equipment.

The Editing Process

Editing software applications and hardware configurations constantly evolve and improve, and excellent instruction on specific editing software and hardware solutions exists on the Web and in printed form. <*www.atomiclearning.com*>, for example, has concise step-by-step audio-visual instructions for beginning and advanced editing techniques.

Many other sources are listed in the appendix of this book. Instead of describing specific programs, commands and file specifications, I want to focus on the student benefits that result from the flow and planning that is part of the editing process.

Let's begin with a quick overview of the post-production phase from beginning to end. There are actually hundreds of tasks and dozens of steps involved in motion picture post-production. For our purposes, I want to look at organizing this phase into eight steps:

"I think the presence of the camera does affect behavior, and you have to acknowledge that. So what we try to do in the editing room is to analyze the footage, and determine whether it's gratuitous mugging for the camera, or whether you're really learning something that's important to the film."
Joe Berlinger

1. Log the Footage
2. Paper Edit
3. Assembly
4. Picture Cut
5. Sound Cut
6. Titles and Finishing
7. Test Screening
8. Export for Viewing

As students evaluate their footage, and as they develop their finished film, one question should be revisited throughout the entire process: "How does this material illustrate what I am trying to say?"

This applies to a shot, a scene and a sequence. It applies to choosing music, adding sound effects and creating titles. It applies to enhancing the image and the use of effects. Editing is really a continual process of analysis, synthesis and communication and this is why it is such a powerful process for students.

When the filming for *Smoke* was over, Linda and I returned to our editing room with many hours of digital video footage. We had footage of the performances themselves as well as a variety of other images. These included establishing shots, close-ups and cutaways.

Now as a filmmaker, my task is to edit this all down to one linear viewable program. "What do I do first?" "Where do I begin?"

The first thing to do is to 'log' the footage.

1. Log the Footage

Logging the footage is about examining what material you have captured during the production stage and identifying it in order to work with it during the editing stage. The completed log list answers the question, "What materials do I have to work with?"

In order to keep track of where all the scenes are located, filmmakers use reference numbers called 'Time Code.' Each frame

Post–Production

of a piece of videotape has an identification number (Time Code) embedded into its digital information. This Time Code is an address that helps editors (and editing software) locate specific footage.

Usually, the tape will automatically begin recording at 00:00:00:00. If the tape was left recording for thirty minutes and fifteen seconds, its Time Code may look like this: 00:30:15:05

The first two numbers (00) represent how many hours from the beginning of the tape the piece is located; in this case, it identifies (because it is a zero) that it is within the first hour.

The next two numbers (30) represent how many minutes into that hour, in this case thirty minutes.

The next two numbers (15) represent how many seconds into that minute, in this case fifteen seconds.

The final two numbers (05) represent how many frames into that second, in this case five frames (There are thirty frames in each second of video).

By using these Time Code numbers, students can document and manage all the footage they have accumulated.

At the very least, a Footage Log is a list of what scenes are where. At its best, and with more time invested, it contains the

Footage Log ■ ■ ■

Title: SMOKE

Log Tape #: 1

Date Recorded: Nov 15

Time	Scene	Take	Comment	
00:00-02:00	1	1	NG (No Good)	Hat blocks Michael in second half
02:15 –03:40	1	2	NG Sound	Airplane overhead
04:00-06:00	1	3	Good	Both performances great

length of each material, comments about the sound, the lighting, the focus, and often answers the question, "Is it interesting?"

On the previous page is a Footage Log from *Smoke*. The log page contains:

- The title of the tape
- The date it was recorded
- The list of all shots recorded
- What each shot is about
- When each shot begins and ends
- Technical notes about each shot
- Aesthetic notes about each shot

Now, having said all this, I must point out that it is not necessary for students to log their footage in order to make a movie. With today's sophisticated desktop editing software you can import your footage from your camera or VCR and have the material appear directly in your editing 'window,' ready to be assembled into the final movie.

But I still recommend that students log their work. The process of watching, analyzing and recording helps familiarize filmmakers with the material that was captured. As you sit in front of a screen and analyze what you recorded, you start to recognize and become more aware of what works and what doesn't.

You learn how handheld shots look versus tripod shots; when a shot is too shaky to use, or when the focus is too soft (out of focus); when a shot is too short in length, or when it goes on for too long. In other words, by analyzing the footage, you become a better capturer of footage next time you have a camera in your hand. You become more fluent with a visual language as you investigate the components that make up the grammar. And this goes back to that idea that filmmaking is a circle and a great example of a continual learning process.

Once you have logged the footage, it is time for a paper edit.

Post-Production

2. Paper Edit

A paper edit consists of identifying, on paper, which shots might best illustrate the idea or tell the story of the film. The list identifies in what order those shots should be seen and exactly what portion of the shot is to be used.

The paper edit uses the Time Code numbers that were recorded during production or during the logging process to identify the specific start and stop points. If a specific start point or end point has not been determined, then an approximate address should still be recorded, as the fine-tuning of each scene will happen later in the post-production process. This list of suggested editing decisions is often referred to as an Edit Decision List (EDL).

While creating their paper edits, students should use their Storyboards, Shot Lists and Scripts as guides and reminders of how the story might be told.

The great thing about paper edits is that they enable students to visualize their film coming together before they sit down at the computer. They have opportunities for developing logic and visualization skills before they begin.

The other great thing about paper edits is that they reduce the amount of time students require on the editing system, since most of the decisions of what to use have already been made.

I would suggest that teachers require students to submit their paper edits before they book time on the editing stations. Why? Because paper edits answer the questions, "Are you prepared?" and, "Do you have an editing plan?"

Here is an example of an Edit Decision List from *Smoke*:

"The greatest amount of time in editing is this process of studying the takes and making notes and struggling to decide which segments you want to use; this takes ten times more time and effort than the actual cutting, which is a very quick process."
Stanley Kubrick

Edit Decision List			■ ■ ■
		Time	
Tape	**In**	**Out**	**Shot Description**
1	00:10:12:10	00:10:22:10	Exterior Smoke Stack
1	00:15:21:15	00:15:26:15	Smoke in Sky
2	00:07:10:10	00:07:14:10	Michael Looking at Smoke
1	00:04:10:10	00:05:00:00	Tyler and Jordan appear

Step 3. Assembly

Assembly refers to the process of putting the film clips that you have decided to use into a linear order from beginning to end. It is an exciting stage because it enables you to see your movie begin to take shape. It is a way to rough out the film and is therefore called a 'rough cut.'

When sculptors set out to carve a statue from a block of marble, they first rough out where the statue's body is before fine-tuning the fingernails. Most editors work in the same way. First they try to get a feel for the video or film in terms of the kind of shots, the kind of pace or the length that it will have. They do not get too concerned with the exact edit point, the titles, the music or sound effects, or the visual cutaways. These will come later.

Technically, the assembly process involves transferring the video footage from the camera into the hard drive of the computer. Today's digital video cameras communicate to the computer with a single 'firewire' cable. This cable connects the video camera and the computer and enables the exchange of digital information to occur in real time; that is, as the video plays back in the camera, it is simultaneously transferred and recorded into the internal or external hard drive of the computer.

Post-Production

The images that are imported are viewed as a series of 'clips' in the editing software window (a clip is a segment taken from a larger portion of video footage). The editor drags those clips into a 'timeline' that displays the order in which they will be viewed. (The timeline is a visual, horizontal display that indicates, usually from left to right, in what order each clip appears.)

A track may consist of video or audio clips, and in some editing systems, there may be hundreds of these 'layers' available. The audio and video tracks, when played simultaneously, combine to present an image on screen and a soundtrack through the speakers.

With the EDL as their guide, editors continue to add the clips that are required until the assembly is complete. At this point, students can watch their entire project, in its assembled form, on the computer screen or on a video monitor. The assembly answers the question, "Are we on the right track?"

Step 4. Picture Cut

The next milestone in the editing process is the picture cut. This point is reached when the film maker is satisfied that all the visual images that are necessary to tell the story are there on the screen in the right order, for the right duration, and with the right visual transitions (cuts, dissolves, wipes, etc.).

As students begin creating scenes, it may be helpful to talk about some of the visual grammar that is involved in scene construction. One way to explore scenes is to consider them as visual paragraphs. In writing, paragraphs often begin with a topic sentence that sets the stage for what the paragraph is about. The body of the paragraph illustrates examples and describes in detail what the paragraph is about, and the closing sentence summarizes the paragraph.

This model can also apply to a scene in a film. Scenes often begin with a shot that establishes where the action takes place

"It's this weird process. I just find the film is being made all through the shooting and even the editing and it's not till we do the final cut that the thing is finally written. I don't actually see films in the way you write a person's film and then you go out and film it and it's done. Each time you bring something new to it, it changes. It's a strange, ad hoc, organic approach to making films. It's the only way I know to work."
Terry Gilliam

and what it is about. Our *Water* project, for example, may contain many scenes. If we were to look at the scene at the water treatment plant, it might be assembled with the following shots:

There may be a shot to establish where the scene takes place or what it is about (or both).

Shot 1 – The exterior of a water treatment plant.

The shots that follow provide the details of what is happening and what the sequence is about.

Shot 2 – Inside the water treatment plant, a wide shot of the machinery at work.

Shot 3 – A medium shot of the plant manager being interviewed.

Shot 4 – A medium shot of a man adjusting a pipe with a wrench.

Shot 5 – A close-up shot of a wrench.

Shot 6 – A medium shot of a woman taking a water sample.

Shot 7 – An extreme close-up shot of water being poured into a test tube.

Shot 8 – The conclusion of the interview.

The end of the scene may have a closing shot that concludes what that scene was about.

Shot 9 – Outside the water treatment plant, a young girl drinks from a water fountain, then runs away, revealing a poster that promotes good water conservation.

These visual paragraphs are built shot by shot into scenes. Scenes are combined into sequences, much like chapters in a book, and then the sequences are combined to tell the entire story from beginning to end.

Post-Production

Step 5. Sound Cut

Once all the images are in place, the next area of attention is the soundtrack. The creation of the soundtrack is as critical as the picture track. Audiences tend to forgive slightly blurry or shaky camera work but seem less likely to forgive poor quality or missing audio. No matter what voyage the eye is taken on, our ears want to hear things clearly. Maybe it's an equilibrium thing, I don't know.

In most Hollywood movies dozens of sound editors, dialogue editors, and music editors will work for many months to produce a rich clean brilliant soundtrack to accompany the picture on screen. These soundtracks may contain over one hundred or more separate tracks of dialogue, sound effects, music, and environmental and atmospheric sounds.

Student editors may want to investigate the potential of the three main components of a well-produced soundtrack:

- Dialogue
- Sound Effects
- Music

Dialogue

Dialogue can refer to the words spoken by the characters in the film or to a section of the film that contains narrated words. These words may have been recorded at the time the scene was recorded or they may have been added later. The process of acquiring those words is referred to as additional dialogue recording (ADR). This can be done as simply as pointing a microphone to an actor or narrator and recording the words. The audio is imported into the editing system and positioned with the corresponding image.

Sometimes the dialogue that is recorded during production is unusable. It may be because the audio level is too low, or because the microphone was not plugged in, or because there was too much other noise in the background. To solve the problem of this unusable dialogue, the filmmaker has the actor watch a video clip of him or herself in a quiet environment and invites them to recite the words again. The actor will repeat the text until the timing of the words on screen match the timing of the actor's new delivery. This is often called 'lip syncing.'

Sound Effects

Sound effects are pieces of audio that enrich the soundtrack. They are often broken down into two categories, those whose source is on the screen, and those whose source is off the screen.

Students can examine what is happening on screen, like water dripping from a tap, a door closing, or a bottle being placed on a table, and augment that action with a sound effect. They can create these effects themselves with a microphone and the camera (or computer) or they can use pre-recorded sound effects available on CDs and web sites.

A class may consider archiving the sound effects created by its sound editors for use in future projects and by future filmmakers.

Students can also use sound effects to create off screen events that the actors may react to, like a telephone ringing, or someone screaming. The physical event off screen may have never taken place, but students discover that events can be believably suggested with the use of the appropriate sound effect at the appropriate time.

in addition, editors often utilize sounds to help create an atmosphere or mood for the scene. A scene that takes place at night may be augmented by the sounds of crickets, and a scene on a football field may benefit from the sounds of

Post-Production

people cheering. The exercise here for students is to imagine what sounds they would hear in that setting, and then add in those layers.

Music

Music is another important part of the soundtrack. There may have been music playing in the background when the scene was recorded, or more likely, students may want to put in music during post-production. Music ties shots together and helps create a flow to the events assembled on screen. It can also be overused. It can be too loud, or distract the viewer's attention from the action on screen and instead of supporting the scene, compete against it.

I encourage experimentation with the music track. One suggestion is to have students select six different styles of music (rock, classical, big band, rap, foreign, pop, for example) and view their project with each of them, noting how each style contributes (or detracts) from the viewing. The same can be done with varying tempos and varying instrumentations.

Music is a significant component of a film project and this exercise can help students understand what characteristics each choice of music suggests and the different atmospheres that can be created through music.

Step 6. *Titles and Finishing*

In the old days of filmmaking, a few years ago, companies that specialized in producing titles supplied filmmakers with opening title sequences and end credit titles. When scenes required the altering of colour, lighting or the addition of special effects, other specialists were called in.

Today, computer-based applications are utilized to conceive

and create the film's title sequence and end credits. In addition, software programs exist to alter colour, lighting and even composition of individual shots and entire scenes.

Students can create titles for their projects in many ways:
- They can use the built-in title-generating feature included in most editing software packages.
- They can create titles in other software applications and then import them into their editing programs.
- They can enlist the help of other talented animation and graphic artists in the school and collaborate with them.

In addition to these digital methods of title creation, consider challenging them to create titles without the aid of any of the above. For example, how can you tie in the title for the *Water* project with the theme of what it is about?

Imagine a large white card with the word WATER painted on it with black felt pen. Place it in the kitchen sink or a bathtub with a few inches of water. Arrange the video camera so it is looking straight down. Start recording. Add in dirty water, bits of garbage, brown or black food colouring, stir it all up and push it over the WATER word without showing your hand.

Now when you look at the footage you will see the word WATER and this strange liquid floating over it, getting increasingly more polluted. The footage can be slowed down or sped up and you can experiment with it until you find a style that would work for the title.

The point of this example is that it is not always about relying on the latest technology to create powerful images. As with every other part of the filmmaking process, low-tech solutions to solve problems are sometimes the most interesting and rewarding.

Step 7. Test Screenings

Many producers incorporate test screenings as part of their post-production process. Filmmakers want to know if audiences understand or can follow what is happening in their films. They also want to see if they have successfully communicated their ideas.

Test screenings can be as simple as showing a film and listening and observing audience reaction, or it can be much more precise, with evaluation forms that audiences fill in based on questions asked by the filmmaker. Sometimes there can be many test screenings after each revision. I suggest utilizing test screenings as part of the filmmaking process in the classroom as a way for students to explore self-evaluations of their work before declaring it complete.

Step 8. Export for Viewing

After the video has been finished on the computer and students have had a chance to finish tweaking, it is time for exporting. Most non-linear editing programs allow you to export from the computer back to the digital camera or to video tape recorders. The same firewire cable that enabled the digital information to flow from the camera to the computer now carries the finished project from the computer to a video recorder or camera.

Ideas Change

When students enter the editing stage of filmmaking, they usually enter with a predetermined idea of what their movie will look like when they finish.

The process of editing is a process of decision making, experimentation and change. Ideas of how a scene was going to be constructed change. Ideas of what scenes should be included will also change. Ideas of how to tell the story, or sometimes, what the story is really about, also change. It is a sometimes-painful process of letting go.

It is difficult to not use a shot that took a lot of time, energy and planning to execute, but if that shot no longer works to illustrate the scene or the idea of the video, then that shot must go.

An interesting exercise is to bring in a DVD of a Hollywood movie and go to the Deleted Scenes section. This is a new phenomenon in watching movies. Now, not only can you see the movie as it was completed, but you can also watch scenes that were deleted from the final film. When I hear the director's commentary, I find it interesting to hear their reasons for leaving out the deleted scenes. Often they will talk about how much work it was to get the shot, or how beautiful it looked, or how great the acting was, or how much they loved it personally, but, ultimately they concede that it slowed down the movie or did not fit with the intent of the sequence or the final film.

I think this is a powerful concept to bring into the classroom. Students should understand that the films they see in the theatres and on television also contain deleted scenes. The removal of 'favourite' material is a process that filmmakers go through in order to reach their ultimate goal of clearly communicating their ideas to an audience. Students should realize that if they are deleting scenes, losing favourite material and have been willing to change their ideas, it might be because they have become real filmmakers, like those on the DVDs.

Ideas change.

Post-Production

16 Premiere

So now the filmmaking is complete. The planning, shooting and editing have resulted in finished movies. The next step is to show these movies to an audience. It is time for a 'premiere' in the classroom. Even though the movies themselves are finished, there is still great opportunity for learning woven into the preparation and presentation of the premiere.

Sense of Accomplishment

It is important for students to show their film to others because of the satisfaction that it brings to them. Observe students as they watch their movies and you will see what I am trying to describe here in words. It is the joy that comes from a feeling of accomplishment. Certainly this feeling is not unique to filmmaking; it can exist when completing any project that requires focus and persistence. It is definitely amplified when the projects reflect the ideas and creative energies of the students involved. And here, in a classroom premiere, that feeling of completion and accomplishment can be proudly acknowledged.

"There are very few films I've made in which there aren't a hundred things I'd like to do differently."
Nicholas Ray

What Do We Need for a Premiere?

A premiere in the classroom can be as simple or sophisticated an event as you wish, or even better, as your students wish.

On a simple level, it can be about setting up a television monitor and viewing the films. But there are so many opportunities for developing higher order thinking skills and creativity in the premiere process that I want to mention some ideas for your consideration.

Planning and Scheduling

First of all, a date has to be set and a plan for the premiere

Distribution

created. Now we find ourselves back to the opportunities and challenges of scheduling and organizing.

- When will we show it?
- How will we show it?
- Where will we show it?
- What order do we show them in and does it matter?
- Who will be invited, if anyone?
- Will there be invitations or posters?

Though perhaps not as demanding as scheduling and planning for the production phase, student imaginations do come up with surprisingly elaborate enhancements for premieres. My suggestion is, if they are willing to organize it, great. Go for it.

Movie Posters and Video Covers

When filmmakers complete their movies, they usually require the talents of a specialized individual or company to distribute their film around the country and around the world. These specialists are called, not surprisingly, distributors. The distributor's objective is to sell the film. How they do this is by the creation of advertising campaigns that include movie posters, television advertising and print media.

The reason I mention distributors and distribution here is that it leads us to another opportunity for learning: the study and production of movie-marketing materials.

Students are familiar with movie advertising as part of the world they live in. They see movie posters every time they go to a cinema, movie advertisements in magazines, movie commercials on television, and even promotional 'trailers' before they get to see the 'main attraction.'

In preparation for the premiere, students can prepare movie-marketing materials for their own movie. What looks at first as a fun little exercise is actually embedded with powerful opportunities and serious investigation of how we are sold ideas and dreams.

"Perhaps it sounds ridiculous, but the best thing that young filmmakers should do is to get hold of a camera and some film and make a movie of any kind at all."
Stanley Kubrick

First the fun part: making a movie poster. The process of making a poster can be as simple as handing out sheets of 11" x 17" paper and asking for posters to be prepared with the date, time and place, and an image from or about the film.

But it can also be a jumping off point for discussion and research on movie posters and other promotional materials whose purpose it is to convince us to go to a cinema or video rental store and put down our hard-earned cash in exchange for the promise of an entertaining experience.

Where this becomes interesting is in the examination of Hollywood marketing materials and the Hollywood movie itself.

One interesting exercise is to obtain a few video covers from a video rental store of movies that students recognize and to deconstruct what and how the packaging materials advertise the film.

- Do they use photographs from the movie?
- Do they use cartoons or drawings?
- Is there any correlation with what is shown on the cover and what is actually in the movie, and if not, why not?
- What words do distributors use to describe and promote the movie?
- How much of the story do they tell, and how do they tell it?

Since media awareness is an important part of preparing students for their world, it seems a great opportunity to have them deconstruct movie advertising as they prepare to construct their own. Hopefully, it is an awareness that will remain with them as they become increasingly exposed to the marketers of the world.

In addition to movie posters, students can also create video covers. Hard shell plastic VHS video covers can be purchased for less than a dollar a piece. If you ask for 'full sleeves,' the video case has a piece of clear plastic which wraps around the front and allows you to slip in apiece of paper (8" x 10" approximately) which becomes the video cover.

"It's really like doing a painting, with a big canvas. You sit there, and you know what you're doing from the start, and as you're doing it, you're painting and it's changing and it's finally done. It took years to get the film finally written and then made and then at the end the film is quite different from what we began with and yet it's exactly the film we set out to make, which is rather strange and paradoxical but it is."
Terry Gilliam

Distribution

Video covers can include information on:

- The creative team
- The duration of the program
- A synopsis of what the program is about
- Images from the production
- Photographs of the creative team on the back cover
- Quotes from people who have seen the movie
- Reasons why people should watch it

In my films there's a competition with the audience to keep ahead of them. I want to break their patterns. I want to shake them up and get them out of those quick, manufactured truths.
John Cassavettes

Popcorn

Finally it is time for popcorn. I like having popcorn at class premieres because it reminds us that the filmmaking process should be about having fun. There's something about munching on popcorn while watching your own movie that completes your filmmaking journey.

Anything to make the event more like a real world premiere is encouraged. Tickets. Programs. Master of ceremonies. Popcorn bags with the school logo attached. Visiting dignitaries. Reporters from the city paper. A red carpet. Formal wear. You get the picture.

Ideas Change

Ok, granted, ideas may not change drastically at this point, and the results of that change may not appear on this particular project. But sometimes they do. I have heard many stories of students watching their work being shown, and then going in the next day and editing one last scene, or deleting, or adding some little detail.

Even if they do not change the project that they have just completed, they may remember to incorporate ideas of what they would have done differently into their next project.

Now let us go in a different direction. Perhaps ideas on how to make their film do not change at all at this stage. Instead, maybe what do change are their ideas on the subject that they have just explored. Perhaps students working on the *Water* video have a greater sense of awareness of the issues relating to conservation, and of the similar challenges of other ecological systems. Perhaps students interviewing people in their community are exposed not only to the facts relating to the subjects, but to the human emotion behind those facts.

This is one of the major student benefits of using filmmaking as a tool for learning, the ability to focus deeply on a subject and to passionately investigate it from every angle.

Spending time with the subject through the planning, production, and post-production phase allows students to gain an awareness and understanding that did not previously exist.

What could be a greater asset for our planet than citizens who are willing to change their ideas, or at least entertain alternate points of view, on issues that affect us all?

Distribution

17 Distribution

We have talked about all the events leading up to the premiere of the filmmaking project in the classroom. Now let us take this even further. Movies created by students are a valuable resource. They demonstrate unique points of view and illustrate students' attitudes towards the world around them. They tell us how the data that surrounds us has been harvested and interpreted by the student.

Thinking in these terms, let us now explore how we can use these resources to further benefit both the students who created them as well as potential audiences.

In this chapter, we explore some of the possibilities and strategies of sharing the students' work with others in their class, their school, their district, their community, and their world.

In the School

We looked at the idea of having a premiere in the classroom, at how much pride and excitement can be generated by the celebration of the creation of the project. Imagine how much pride and excitement could be generated by sharing the movies with the whole school.

Here are some ideas:

- Set up a resource section in each classroom with student-created videos available for viewing and signing out.
- Set up a section of your school library with videos created by students at that school.
- Incorporate videos for screening at assemblies.
- Have television monitors showing student videos during parent interviews, open houses and sporting events.
- Create a schedule of noon-hour screenings of student videos, and make sure to post that screening list everywhere.

I want the audience to take away a full stomach. I like the idea of leaving explosive shards somewhere in their brains. Things that they can't forget that will stay with them for years."
Terry Gilliam

Distribution

In the School District

Let's take it out of the school. Look for opportunities to share these resources with other schools in the district.

- Create a database of film by subject, student, date or curriculum, and circulate it to other schools as a resource list that they can use. Encourage other schools to do the same. Use the Web to update and share information. Web sites could be created that contain movie details, previews or perhaps the entire film.
- Create a film festival in your district and recognize excellence in video production.
- Use films to augment inter-district debating teams by having film debates.

In the Community

Let us take it outside the school walls. Can these films be exhibited to your community? One approach is to invite the community to view an evening of films, perhaps grouped by theme or class, and hold the event in your auditorium, gym or studio.

Another approach is to take the films into the community itself. One of the ways that filmmaking can be even more valuable to our students is to use it to create bridges outside the school, and one of those bridges is to the community.

Partnerships between business, community groups and schools are even more necessary today as all three stretch to use increasingly dwindling resources. How can schools partner with groups outside the school to highlight student-created films?

Some ideas:

- Show them at local banks while people wait in line.
- Show them at hospitals, in waiting rooms, or have them available in rooms.
- Show them at gatherings like national holidays.
- Show sports-related films at community sporting events.
- If the films are about multiculturalism, get in touch with the local multicultural society and arrange to have a

display booth playing during their events.

- Show them to other learning organizations and community groups.
- If the film is about someone in the community, like an artist, it could be playing at an art gallery.
- If the film is about something of interest to all the community, like the *Water* film, see if it can be played at City Hall. (And don't forget to give a copy to the kind folks who helped out at the water treatment plant).

In addition to actually showing the films, the process of going into the community, making contacts, creating awareness, and marketing the events where the films will be shown can be another great learning opportunity for students.

There are many places where student films can play in the community. The key is to look at the topic of the film and the theme that it explores and to find a compatible community organization or event to intertwine with, and then to pursue it!

Broadcasts

Another opportunity for reaching audiences beyond the school is to broadcast the films on television. Now it becomes even more exciting for the students as the results of their work are shared on a medium that they are very familiar with.

There are many schools that work with local community broadcasters that allow time each week for student videos. More adventurous broadcasters integrate the students into the design and production of each weekly show and in this way give students hands-on experience in producing weekly television.

Begin with making contact with the local community station, or have the students make contact, and explore to what extent they can participate. In my experience, they are always looking for new things to show on their networks, so it is worthwhile to persistently investigate their potential.

The great thing about students' films being broadcast on

"I think in some ways the most joy that you get out of the artistic process is believing that somehow you're getting better by doing it and that hopefully other people are getting better by watching it."
Jodie Foster

Distribution

television is that students start reaching a wide audience. Feedback from the audience should be encouraged through on-screen email addresses, web site addresses and phone numbers. Receiving that feedback can be a very powerful lesson for students in understanding firsthand the relationship and responsibilities between those who create media and those who respond to it.

Awareness Campaigns

Again, there are more opportunities for learning in this process. Once a broadcaster is found, and an air date is determined, you can develop an awareness campaign to let people know that the film will be on the air. Here are some ways:

- Create posters
- Create a Press Release
- Create a Press Kit
- Create Electronic Press Kits
- Arrange for interviews with local newspapers, radio stations and television stations

Press Kits

Filmmakers use a communication and marketing tool called a Press Kit. In the same way, if students or student teams would like to publicize their film, or create awareness that their film is being shown in the school, or community or on television, they should consider creating a Press Kit.

Press Kits contain information about the project. This may include:

- Where and when the film is playing
- A synopsis of what the film is about
- A copy of the script or a transcription from the finished film
- Written information about the students who created it
- Overviews of the learning outcomes addressed by the project

- Short stories of how the films were made, including how obstacles were overcome
- 'Behind the scenes' photographs of the making of the film
- Still images from the finished project
- Key artwork (The Key Art is the one image that the filmmaker utilizes to represent their project on press kits, posters, and advertisements.)
- Reviews from people who have seen the movie

Electronic Press Kits

With today's digital technologies, paper-based press kits are often replaced with Electronic Press Kits or EPKs. These electronic press kits may be delivered as videotapes, CD-ROMs, DVDs or web sites.

They often include all the material in the press kits plus additional material including:
- Film highlights
- Behind the scenes film footage showing how it was made
- Video interviews with the director, actors and others

With non-linear media delivery technologies (CD, DVD, Web), all the above information can be presented through an on-screen menu that allows for easy access to the project material. This makes it easier for the people working in the press to access and utilize information about the film. If you give them everything they need to tell your story, it increases the chance that they will want to assist with the awareness campaign.

These Press Kits become both a scrapbook of the production as well as another example of a communication tool.

Producers usually hire 'publicists' to organize and interface with the media. Perhaps when roles are assigned, when the duties of director, editor, and cameraman are defined, there is someone who takes the role of publicist. The publicist's duties are to make sure that information is gathered, photographs are

Distribution

taken, interviews are recorded, story synopses are constructed, and the whole thing comes together in a clear and understandable presentation like the press kits and EPKs.

Film Festivals

When I was working with a grade three class producing *The Princess and the Street Kid*, one of the first things they asked was, "Can we put this into a film festival?" I don't think I even knew what a film festival was when I was in the third grade. Today's students are much more media savvy then I was as a student. They know that film festivals exist; they know that it is a chance to show their work to a large audience, and to show their work to an audience outside of where they call home. This is all very exciting.

Timberline Secondary is a school in Campbell River, British Columbia, that set out to make a twelve-minute film about the graduated learning program that is available in British Columbia schools. An honours media program was developed where a team of students from multiple grades undertook to produce an informative project aimed at high school students who were interested in the driving awareness and safety program that was introduced. The goal was to produce a video that could be seen around British Columbia schools and to educate their student peers around the province as to the details of this course.

When it was completed, they submitted it to a film festival in Toronto and were awarded the best student documentary at the Canadian International Annual Student Film Festival.

And so again, here is an example of how a project can not only achieve its original goals, but also develop students' self-confidence and self-esteem as they see their film productions recognized locally, nationally and internationally.

The Backyard Film Festival <*www.backyardfilmfestival.com*> is an example of one of the many student film festivals that is always welcoming submissions.

The World Wide Web

Recent years have seen giant leaps in digital technologies and the Internet. These innovations will continue exponentially, and soon we will be able to send, view and download full screen, crystal clear digital movies over the Internet.

Many schools have already found great success with posting student videos on school web sites. It is an inexpensive method of getting students' work shown to a large audience, and it elicits viewer feedback from around the world.

When students create web pages that show their movies, they have an opportunity to develop visual marketing skills as they conceive how the site will look. They also can exercise their technical skills as they design how the site will work, how the files will be stored, and how the movies will be viewed.

One of the goals of *<www.thedirectorintheclassroom.com>* web site is to be a catalyst for the sharing of student filmmaking projects over the Internet. Please check it out.

DVD

Digital Versatile Discs, or Digital Video Discs (DVD) can now be created on personal desktop computers at a relatively affordable price. These optical discs allow much more storage than CD-ROMs.

What this means to filmmakers is that approximately one hour and a half of digital video can be stored on each DVD. This creates an opportunity for an entire class project of videos to be stored on one or two discs.

Their random access design enables viewers to select the project they want to view instantly. Students can create menus that can guide the viewer to additional information related to their movies, as discussed previously in the section on electronic Press Kits.

Because they can be played back on a home DVD unit, they can be signed out of the class or library and viewed at home or in other facilities.

Distribution

Ideas Change

As students show their work around the school, in their communities, and around the world, they begin experiencing the relationship between filmmaker and audience.

What is so thrilling about student videos being distributed and presented to audiences is that students realize they have a voice and that their voice can be far reaching.

They will receive feedback from the people who see it and discover that the movie they have made has created avenues of discussion. Audiences may agree or disagree, like or dislike the project, but regardless, they will somehow be affected.

As students listen to audience feedback and consider it in relation to the ideas they proposed in their video, they now have the ability to compare the two, and to, even slightly, allow their ideas to change once more.

"He (Woody) always says the same thing after each movie: "That was great. Now take a bigger risk." About Woody Allen

Pause, Reflect and Advance....

Stop. Relax. Breathe. Congratulations!

One of the most rewarding steps in the filmmaking process is this last step, which is about stopping to look back and reflect on the adventure that just occurred. There needs to be an opportunity for exhaling, for getting out the frustrations, and for celebrating the victories of overcoming all the challenges. It should be more than a clinical analysis of each step or each project. It should be about the emotional explorations that were taken and asking the question, "What was learned?"

What Did We Learn?

Consider having students write a page or two examining the question, "What did we learn?" You may want to be more specific and ask what was learned about the subject they were studying, about the filmmaking process, working in teams, researching, communicating ideas generally or about themselves. Or you may want to keep it undefined and see what happens, see what surprises they release. Experiment!

In evaluating the filmmaking process itself, consider having the students create a database about filmmaking do's and don'ts based on their experiences. Place it on a web site or a classroom computer and have the results of their observations become a living legacy to help future filmmakers. This brings us to the idea of students as mentors.

Students as Mentors

As students develop an understanding of technical and thinking skills involved in filmmaking, they themselves become another great resource for teaching and learning.

Recently, I recruited two˙ grade twelve students that I had worked with to help a grade six class with their editing. It was a

"At the moment, while I think the technology of film-making has improved and expanded enormously, I think that the basic questions of story and character have suffered. I would be happy to see the time come when problems are set up and solved in human terms so that an audience can walk out not only having been entertained but left with something that will improve them as human beings and will improve the world they live in."
Vincent Sherman

great experience for the grade six class to have these senior mentors come in and work with them, and it was great to see the grade twelve students working as mentors with the younger students. The older students commented that they were surprised at the high quality of the production that the younger students accomplished, and the younger students really enjoyed teaming up with these older students who shared the same interest in filmmaking as them.

Explore opportunities in your school and district for these mentoring experiences. Have students create a web site which lists what is happening in your class, school or area related to student filmmaking production. Is there a way to match experienced students with filmmakers who are just starting out?

These mentoring opportunities can be one-time short-term instruction, or ideally, they are a longer duration that encourages a deeper relationship between mentor and student.

Create bridges between different classrooms and schools. Create bridges between age groups. Create bridges between those who know and those who hunger to learn.

A Time to Dream

Now that students have had a chance to see their ideas evolve into movies that reach audiences, it is time to ask the most important question, "What do they want to do next?" This is where we started, back in Chapter 8, when we started examining the kind of video projects that we want students to explore. Now that students and teachers have had a chance to experience the filmmaking process from beginning to end, it is a great time to imagine what could be done or what should be done next.

Perhaps it calls for a group brainstorming session or perhaps it is about individual reflection. Whatever you decide, try to include some time to dream of what would be a great follow-up project.

Ideas Change …the World

"Never doubt that a small group of committed citizens can change the world. Indeed, it's the only thing that has."
– Margaret Meade

Now, at the end of the process we can really talk about how ideas change…the world.

By now, students have turned their ideas into plans, their plans into action and their actions into results. They have communicated these ideas to audiences around the community and around the world. They have worked in teams, created strategies, refined goals, discovered resources and overcome obstacles. They began with the intangible and finished with the tangible.

Now, as they approach their next film, their next project or their next challenge, they will bring with them real world skills and experiences to help them succeed.

Ideas change, and the most important ideas to change are ideas about themselves. Imagine if they realized that they are the people who can make change happen.

When students stop being passive observers of their world and discover that they have the powerful potential to positively affect their society, to challenge what they dislike and what they believe unjust, to defend what they love, and to argue passionately for a cause, then we have truly succeeded in providing them with an education relevant and critical for the success and survival of their own lives and of their planet.

Part 3:

Obstacles are Opportunities

"If I'd gone to film school, I would have never known something like El Mariachi was possible. In fact, I would have laughed at the idea and said it was impossible. Don't be told something is impossible. There's always a way."
Robert Rodriguez

"It is kind of fun to do the impossible."
Walt Disney

19: Assessment of Film Projects

Obstacle

Movies are art and art is subjective. How can the assessment of film projects move from the subjective to the objective? What kind of feedback can be provided to assist students with improving ideas and techniques for exploring and learning through film production? And, how can we put a number on projects driven by creativity and passion?

Opportunity

One suggestion is to think of the film assessment as a movie review. We talked earlier about how movie reviewers look at the individual components in an attempt to create objective evaluations.

In this chapter we will look at:
- Film reviews as rubrics
- An example of a basic film rubric
- An example of a more detailed film rubric
- Who the film reviewers might be

Film Reviews as Rubrics

The last time you saw a film, do you remember discussing it with someone else who saw it, but having two different points of view of how it affected you or what it was trying to say? This is the challenge of analyzing any creative student project: each student filmmaker's perspective and efforts are true to that student, yet, in the educational world that we live in, some kind of assessment is required.

For this reason, one suggestion in discussing assessment with students is to first talk about film reviews in the real world. Ask for a suggestion of a film that most of them have seen, and have them write a paragraph review of that film. What did they like, or what did they not like?

Is there a unanimous decision? Probably not. Why not? Because we all have different ideas of what we like and don't like when we watch a film. This can be explored further in a classroom discussion and provide a great introduction to designing their own assessment criteria.

Alternatively, have students bring in one film review from the Web, a magazine or a newspaper, and have them dissect what the reviewer liked or disliked, in terms of different categories. Build a list from everyone's input.

This may include the reviewers' comments on:

- the story
- the believability of the plot
- acting style and techniques
- cinematography
- the use of sound
- the use of music
- editing
- the visual design and look of the sets, wardrobe and effects
- their own objective impression of the overall film

With this as an example, discuss how students can design an assessment tool for their own movies. What categories from the above should or should not be included? Also, what additional categories should be included that would demonstrate that the subject of their learning exploration was understood?

The challenge remains of how to maintain an appreciation for creativity. My niece recently handed in a paper in her science class that was a study of whales. In it, she compared how she and her friends resemble a pod of whales—how they are similar and different in the way they move, communicate and play.

Her perspective was fresh and the content interesting but she received a poor mark. Ultimately, it is the personal preference of each educator as to how they will recognize and acknowledge fresh perspectives, and then how they will translate student creativity into a grade.

Perhaps it is the very elusiveness of any kind of creativity benchmark that can make this type of assessment so perplexing.

A Basic Film Assessment Rubric

Following are some of the many rubrics that are on our web site <www.thedirectorintheclassroom.com>. Please feel free to adapt them to your specific requirements. These detailed rubrics relate to the filmmaking process and do not specify curriculum content, as it will vary with each grade and with each project.

However, a blank form is included on the CD and the appendix lists several great reference sites on developing rubrics for curriculum content.

The rubric for content is ultimately the most important part of the assessment. A flashy film alone does not demonstrate deep understanding. Regardless of the sophistication or the exemplary nature of the finished film production, the key question is, "What has been learned, if anything, about the subject being explored?"

Who is Assessing?

The rubrics are suggestions for designing an assessment strategy. Please experiment!

By having distinct categories of evaluation, the person who is performing the assessment can objectively analyze some or all of these questions and criteria.

But who is performing the assessment? Teachers should make it clear to students when they start who will be assessing the projects and what they will be basing their assessments on.

The assessments may be performed by the:

- Teacher
- Students
- An outside party

Most teachers are comfortable with carrying out the assessment themselves using the rubrics that they, or they and their students, designed. But another idea is for the students themselves, or the students working with the teacher, to evaluate the film pieces, based again on the evaluation criteria that was set forth in the project's initial goals and descriptions.

Further, if two classes were producing film works, is it possible that the different classes could evaluate each other's work? Or is it possible that someone in the community could be involved in evaluating the work, like a filmmaker, an artist, or a scientist who could bring in their own perspectives?

Projects that live beyond the teacher's desk will have more sense of purpose for students and their enthusiasm for producing the video (and for learning) will be sparked by the connection to the world outside the classroom.

My point is that, just as the process of filmmaking brings with it new ideas on how we teach and how we learn, it also brings with it an invitation to explore brand new methods of assessment. This is a challenging and I think necessary part of keeping up with learning in the 21st century.

Rubric One • Basic Film Assessment ■ ■ ▢

	Developing (1)	Competent (2)	Exemplary (3)	SCORE
Idea and Information	• Ideas are unclear • Ideas are incomplete • Information is unorganized	• Ideas are clear • Ideas are complete • Information is organized	• Ideas are expressed in a creative manner • Ideas are thoroughly explored • Information is organized and presented in a creative manner	
Narration/Performance	• Narrator rushes through or drags behind on screen images • Narration is dry, without emotion or change in inflection	• Narration has a good pace to match visuals • Emotion and inflection appropriate to on-screen images	• Good pace and innovative use of narration • Narration uses a variety of inflection, pace and emotion	
Camera	• Image is usually out of focus • Image is usually unsteady	• Image is usually in focus • Image is usually steady	• Image is always in focus • Image is always steady • Innovative use of camera	
Sound	• Sound is unclear • Voices can not be heard • Music is too loud	• Sound is clear • Voices can be heard • Music is not too loud	• Innovative use of voice, sound effects or music	
Goals	• Did not accomplish the goals and objectives outlined for this project	• Accomplished most of the goals and objectives outlined for this project	• Accomplished all of the goals and objectives outlined for this project	
			Sub-Total	/(15)

Rubric Two • Development & Pre-production

	Developing (1)	Competent (2)	Exemplary (3)	SCO
Script	• Relies entirely on dialogue and narration to tell story • One person wrote the Script, without input from the rest of the group • Does not explore the defined subject	• Combines dialogue, narration and the use of images • Some collaboration • Explores the defined subject	• Rich in images and sparse on expository narration and dialogue • Created in collaboration with all of the members of the group • Explores the defined subject with creative perspectives	
Pitching	• No preparation put into presentation • Inaudible • Unsure of story	• Well prepared • Good oral presentation skills • Demonstrates an understanding of the story to be filmed	• Very prepared, story memorized and delivered without a Script • Excellent use of voice, pacing and emotion to pitch story • Thorough understanding of story • Use of audio visual aids	
Storyboard	• No Storyboard was created or no effort was put into its creation • No audio notations • No scene descriptions	• Storyboard was created • The use of audio was sometimes indicated • Scene descriptions were included	• Storyboard clearly described each shot • Audio ideas indicated and well thought out • Innovative use of camera angles, lens choices and movement • Scene descriptions were articulate	
Planning	• No Cast/Crew List • No Scene Breakdown • No Schedule • No ideas for locations • No Equipment List	• Cast/Crew List partially completed • Some scenes have breakdowns • Some scheduling was considered • Some locations was considered • Some equipment considerations	• Cast/Crew List completed • Detailed Scene Breakdown • Detailed Schedule • Detailed Location Plan • Detailed Equipment List	
Teamwork	• One person did most or all of the work	• The group members participated in their respective roles	• Members contributed towards the project's success in their own roles and helped with other roles' objectives outlined for this project	
			Sub-Total	

ubric Two (cont.) • Production

	Developing (1)	Competent (2)	Exemplary (3)	SCORE
ipment	• Did not use any locations, was all shot in a classroom • Did not handle equipment safely	• Arranged for most of the required equipment • Handled equipment safely	• Arranged for all of the equipment • Handled equipment safely	
ation	• Did not arrange for equipment • Did not phone ahead	• Utilized a location • Phoned ahead, arranged for access	• Creative use of locations • Phoned ahead, arranged access and sent thank you cards to location contacts	
anization	• Not well organized • Unable to record • Lack of planning documents (Shot List, Script or Storyboards)	• Organized • Recorded scenes • Brought one planning document with them to set (Shot List, Script or Storyboards)	• Well organized • Filming objectives realized • Brought more than one planning document with them to set (Shot List, Script, Storyboards)	
era	• Unable to operate camera • Used only one type of shot • Camera did not move (No dolly, crane or handheld)	• Able to operate camera • Used more than two types of shots • One kind of camera movement was used	• Demonstrated camera proficiency • Used a variety of camera angles • Explored a variety of camera movements	
ting	• Unable to see image	• Able to see image clearly	• Innovative use of lighting	
io	• Unable to record sound • No audio on tape	• Able to record sound • Audio was usually clear	• Demonstrated good audio recording skills • Audio was always clear	
nwork	• One person did most or all of the work	• The group members participated in their respective roles	• Members contributed to the project's success in their own roles and helped with other roles	
			Sub-Total	**(21)**

Rubric Two (cont.) • Post–production

	Developing (1)	Competent (2)	Exemplary (3)	SC
Editing – Organization	• No paper edit prepared • Did not arrange for time at editing station • Could not locate source tape	• List of shots prepared • Booked time on editing station • Able to locate source tapes	• Proper Edit Decision List prepared including In and Out points • Booked time on editing station • Able to locate source tapes	
Editing – Video	• There was no consideration of pacing the editing to the subject, image or audio • None of the shots had been trimmed; they were left as they were shot • Did not use a variety of shots (wide, medium, close-ups) to describe a scene	• There was some consideration of pacing the editing to the subject, images and audio • Some shots were trimmed • Some use of wide shots, medium shots and close-ups to describe a scene	• Editing had good pace appropriate to the subject, the image and the audio throughout • All shots were trimmed; with clean In and Out points • Good use of wide shots, medium shots and close-ups to describe a scene	
Editing – Audio	• No audio editing • No use of music • No use of sound effects • No use of atmosphere (Not all movies demand music, sound effects or atmosphere, so this is included only if the project description requests it)	• Audio editing • Use of music • Use of sound effects • Use of atmosphere (Not all movies demand music, sound effects or atmosphere, so this is included only if the project description requests it)	• Good audio editing • Good use of music • Good use of sound effects • Good use of atmosphere (Not all movies demand music, sound effects or atmosphere, so this is included only if the project description requests it)	
Editing – Titles & Transitions	• No titles were used • Cuts only editing, no transitions were used	• Titles were used • Some transitions used but poorly executed	• Creative use of titles • Transitions used and well executed	
Teamwork	• One person did most or all of the editing	• There was some collaboration	• All members of the group were involved in the decision-making process and had a chance for hands-on editing	
			Sub-Total	
			TOTAL	

20: Copyright and Other Thorny Issues

Disclaimer: The author is not an attorney and this article may not be substituted for formal legal advice from a Board attorney well versed in school law and copyright law.

Obstacle

Living in a digital age has made the downloading, exchanging and manipulation of digital images, audio and text effortless. This very ease of use, however, is often enjoyed without regard for the ownership or intent of the media's original creator.

We want to encourage students to go outside the classroom and bring the world into their learning, and for their videos to be rich in visual and audio imagery, but an obstacle becomes apparent: How do you encourage the use of digital photos, digital video, music and other elements into filmmaking and still respect permission, copyright and other issues?

Opportunity

There are at least two opportunities here for students:

- They can create original works.
- They can explore the world of copyright, fair use and permission, gain an understanding and an insight into the issues surrounding those topics, and then choose to work or not work within those rules.

I worked on a feature film where my role as one of the producers was to handle all the issues surrounding copyright, permission, and slander. It was a fascinating responsibility because it opened up my eyes to the whole world of getting permission. Everything in the movie had to be 'cleared.' In the filmmaking sense, clearing means:

- To have permission to use something which does not belong to you for the purpose of making the movie.

- To be assured that the information presented will not invite a challenge of ownership, defamation, slander or other potential lawsuit.

How much 'clearing' can occur? For the one feature film, I had a shelf full of three-ring binders.

Title

First of all, the title of the feature film had been previously registered with an unrelated production company and so there was much back and forth between law firms about whether we could, or if we should, use our original title. In the end, we changed our title to avoid a potential lawsuit.

For student productions, this should not be a problem; however, if a program is being broadcast or exhibited outside the classroom, it may cause concerns if it slanders or refers to a recognized title of a movie, book, television show or other product. The safest approach is to avoid any connection. The next safest approach is to explore fair use polices for multimedia and come to your own conclusions based on each project and its use.

A great site for details of the fair use policy exists at: <*www.libraries.psu.edu/mtss/fairuse/default.html*>. There is a friendlier distillation by Hal Davidson at: <*www.mediafestival.org/copyrightchart.html*>.

The Script

In order for a producer to insure a production, the insurance company will request that the Script undergo a script clearance report. This report, which usually costs many thousands of dollars, examines every word, name, song, image, audio reference and location mentioned in the script and suggests what kind of permission (clearance) be obtained.

The report usually advises that the use of actual products, recognizable voices and characters, and items protected by copyright be avoided. Incidental references in the script to actual persons, places or things are not noted unless the reference has possible derogatory information. With these results in hand, the producer can set about clearing each item that the report suggests.

I suggest that, prior to filming, students should go through their scripts and clear them as well. Specifically, they should ensure that there is no defamatory language or characterization that could be perceived as slanderous. Slander can be described as the act of saying something false or malicious that damages somebody's reputation. Dangerously close to slander, but somehow protected by society, is parody.

Parody is found in a piece of music, a piece of writing or in a film that deliberately copies another work in a comic or satirical way. *Mad* magazine and *Saturday Night Live* are examples of parody from our media culture.

I have seen some wonderful parodies of commercial products, movies and television shows that have emerged out of the brilliant minds of student filmmakers, and, which I felt were appropriate as a tool for dissecting media and raising media awareness. Video can be a powerful tool and should be wielded accordingly. Perhaps there is an excellent opportunity for a classroom discussion on the differences between slander and parody so that students can really comprehend the difference in intent.

Photographs

Our feature film was set in the 1960s and one of the scenes had a teacher giving a slide show in a university lecture hall. The images on screen were to be from black and white images from the Civil Rights movement. Selections were made from various stock photo libraries and news service archives, and each of the final photographs selected was individually negotiated to determine a usage price. The usage price, or 'rights payment,' was determined by the popularity of the image, the photographer, as well as, by the market of the film. We negotiated for unlimited use around the world, in theatres, television and other media, and the agreed-upon price was around seven hundred dollars per image. Because of this expense, there was a determination to use only the images that were absolutely critical. We looked at ways to shoot our own black and white photos to mix in with the originals, to stretch our budget further.

For student filmmakers, it is easy to download images from the Internet and incorporate them into their videos. The problem is, of course, that most of the images are taken without consideration of permission. There are several solutions.

1. Use Royalty Free Photographs

These are photographs which the owner or photographer has granted permission for use in schools. Some restrictions may apply to their use outside the school, so it's always a good idea to read the fine print.

A great source for thousands of royalty free photographs is: *<www.pics4learning.com>*. At this site, there is a searchable database to find specific images, a listing of over thirty categories and links to copyright friendly sites that include images from NASA, the Civil War, the Depression Era and a wide variety of other sites.

2. Get Permission

Have students track down the photographer or the owner of the image that they want to use. Have them compose and send a request stating their intent and why they would like to use the photo in their video. Either they will receive permission or they will not. If they do not, it becomes another opportunity for problem solving. How can a student get the idea of this image into their film? Is there another photo that they could use? Can they create their own?

3. Create Your Own

When in doubt, there is nothing like creating your own images to be absolutely sure that you can use it in your video. But beyond the convenience of giving oneself permission, taking your own photographs becomes another opportunity for creating and using visual media.

Stock Footage

One of the scenes called for dramatic footage of California surfers. We had the option of creating the scene ourselves or using existing (stock) footage from that era. We located great 1960s surfing footage from a film library *<www.grinberg.com>* and were able to use it in our film for a fraction of the cost of sending out a film crew, actors and equipment.

Students can also use stock footage in their own video productions. Some companies now offer royalty free film collections for use in teaching and learning. These 'stock' film clips can become part of a classroom reference collection.

A great opportunity for students is to create their own stock footage collections. After their film projects have been completed, what happens to the original footage? Selected shots can be transferred from one DV cassette to another, or edited together and stored on DV tape, CD or DVD. A database could be created that would identify what footage exists in the "Royalty Free Classroom Archives" and perhaps provide a thumbnail or low-resolution sample. Perhaps these databases could be posted on the Web and shared with other schools. A student in Saskatoon, Saskatchewan could trade films with a student in New York City and have access to footage that each student would find impossible to record him or herself.

TV Clips

The film I was producing also included a scene where the actors were watching television in their hotel room. Each of the video clips that appeared on screen had to be cleared. Some clips were commercials, movies, television programs and broadcaster identification spots. Every time you watch a movie and you see a character watching television or going to a movie theatre, you can be assured that the movie they are watching has been cleared, and that permission has been granted or usage rights have been paid.

Students love to use bits of pieces of movies and commercials in their productions. They import them from videos they have rented, recordings they have made from television, or clips they have downloaded from the Web.

As with still photographs, permission is required to used copyrighted materials. There is much gray area in the discussion of fair use policies; where and when materials can be used. Again, I point to the previously mentioned web site as an introduction to the discussion of the fair use guidelines.

Music

In the feature film I helped produce, music played a big part in recreating the 1960s atmosphere on screen. I had to research the ownership rights for every song that we wanted to use. Most songs have more than one kind of rights attached to them.

There are rights for the lyrics and the music referred to as 'publishing' rights, and then there are rights for the performance of an artist often called 'recording' rights.

The seven songs from the 1960s came in at a budget of over

$100,000. Buddy Holly's "*True Love Ways*" for example, cost $15,000 for publishing rights and $15,000 for recording rights. In an attempt to use more songs in the soundtrack, we had some of the classic songs re-recorded by contemporary artists, so that we only paid for the publishing rights. The newly recorded songs proved quite successful and became a good selling soundtrack CD.

I mention this story, because the same applies for students. Problem solving and creativity apply to all parts of the filmmaking process, and here, in the use of music, the opportunities remain. Students may want to use a song from their CD collection, which may be acceptable under the fair use policies, but it will limit where they can show their work.

Instead, here are some suggestions:

1. Use Royalty Free Music

This is music that has been created for use in educational settings and which requires no further permission or fees for use past the original cost of licensing or purchase. They can be purchased as collections, in categories (comedy, drama, adventure, etc.), or as individual music clips on web sites. Here are a few sources, with many more at <*www.thedirectorintheclassroom.com*>:

- www.smartsound.com
- www.sounddogs.com
- www.pbtm.com
- www.royaltyfreemusic.com

2. Get Permission

It is possible to track down the owner of the rights to a recorded piece of music from the information on a CD cover or through web sites; therefore, it is also possible for students to ask permission to use that music in their film.

Although it requires some detective work, patience and planning, it is possible and it has been done. It is also a great exercise that makes a human connection between students and the music industry.

In the feature film that I was clearing, there was a scene where one of the young boys was reading a *Mad* magazine. I had to track down a copy of the magazine, call up their office, and ask to speak to the publisher. I spoke with William M. Gaines himself, and could not help telling him that I was a big fan, and that I had grown up reading his magazine. We spoke about the film we were making and how we wanted to have his magazine in the scene. He gave his permission and we spoke a little longer on life, filmmaking and *Mad*.

After I hung up the phone, I realized that I had just finished speaking with this celebrity who for many years was only a name on a paper to me. Suddenly, the world became smaller, more attainable and a little less overwhelming.

3. *Creating Original Music*

Students can create their own music. They can record themselves or others performing original music and lyrics. Or they can inquire into having others in the school create original music for their films. As well, they can approach musicians or bands in the community and see if they are interested in creating some original music for their videos. Most bands or musicians will already have their original works recorded on cassette or CD and here is an opportunity for students to collaborate with musical professionals in their community.

Sonicfire Pro, <*www.smartsound.com*>, is an interesting software solution that enables students to take royalty free music and then change its length and qualities to match their film. It provides a window on screen in which the students' film can be viewed, and to which the music can be cued. For example, if the scene starts with a wide shot of a building and then cuts to someone running down the stairs, a student may want to use two different kinds of music for each shot. They can import the film, play the music, change the duration of the music, and then place the music in exactly the spot where the shot changes. In addition, the instrumentation and qualities of the music can be explored and altered.

What I like about these features is the ability for students to experiment with the different musical approaches to scoring their films. I also like that the ability to create music electronically may interest and introduce them to the world of music itself. Perhaps it might bring more relevance and urgency to those gruelling hours of practicing scales in music class.

4. Public Domain

Public domain refers to compositions that are not covered by copyright and therefore able to be arranged, reproduced, performed, recorded or published. For example, the song "*Camptown Races*" was originally copyrighted in 1850, but the copyright has now lapsed so it is said to be in the public domain. Theoretically, students could record a version of that song for their video without fees or permission. However, as with everything in this chapter, rules can be interpreted in various ways, and I urge you and students to explore specific meanings and interpretations with the specifics of each project.

There is an excellent reference site regarding the use of public domain songs and music at *<www.pdinfo.com>*.

Permission

The motion picture industry is big on 'getting permission' and I think it offers good guidance for students to follow when making their own films. On the CD, there are some examples for your use. Please check with your own School Board attorneys before using them in the classroom.

There are permission slips, called 'Releases' for:

- Actors (to use for students and others whose voice or image appears on the program)
- Locations (to acknowledge permission that filming may take place at a particular location with the consent of the location's owner)
- Materials (to acknowledge the authorized use of audio, video, photographs or other media in student videos)

Summary

The more original the work, the less paperwork involved. Encourage solutions to copyright issues through creative problem solving and original ideas!

21: Meeting SCANS Goals

The Secretary's Commission on Achieving Necessary Skills (SCANS) was appointed by the Secretary of Labor of the United States to determine the skills our young people need to succeed in the world of work. The Commission's fundamental purpose is to encourage a high-performance economy characterized by high-skill, high-wage employment.

The report suggested a three-part foundational strategy and targets five workplace competencies that should be considered in curriculum. This chapter examines how the process of filmmaking includes opportunities to address all of these goals.

I include this chapter in this book because although the report was created in the United States, I believe the future skills that are detailed would benefit students from any country. Perhaps this correlation between filmmaking and future skills can be used as ammunition to justify to administers and boards why educators should be supported with filmmaking equipment in their class-rooms and filmmaking projects in their teaching. The Three-Part Foundation involves:

1. **Basic Skills**
   - Reading
   - Writing
   - Arithmetic /Mathematics
   - Listening
   - Speaking

2. **Thinking Skills**
   - Creative Thinking
   - Decision Making
   - Problem Solving
   - Seeing Things in the Mind's Eye
   - Knowing How to Learn
   - Reasoning

Three-Part Foundation (continued.)...

3. Personal Qualities
- Responsibility
- Self-esteem
- Sociability
- Self-management
- Integrity/Honesty

The Five Workplace Competencies:
- Resources
- Interpersonal
- Information
- Systems
- Technology

Basic Skills ■ ■ ■

SCANS	**Filmmaking**

Learners read, write, perform arithmetic and mathematical operations, listen and speak.

Reading

Learners locate, understand, and interpret written information in prose and in documents such as manuals, graphs and schedules.

Writing

Learners communicate thoughts, ideas, information, and messages in writing; and create documents such as letters, directions, manuals, reports, graphs and flow charts.

Arithmetic/Mathematics

Learners perform basic computations and approach practical problems by choosing appropriately from a variety of mathematical techniques.

Listening

Learners receive, attend to, interpret, and respond to verbal messages and other cues.

Speaking

Learners organize ideas and communicate orally.

Students develop skills by:

Development
- Reading and responding to project goals and criteria
- Listening and speaking during brainstorming of ideas

Pre-production
- Developing oral presentation skills through pitching
- Locating, understanding and interpreting research information
- Communicating thoughts, ideas and information through Storyboards, Scripts and Shot Lists
- Creating Budgets that require basic computations and a variety of mathematical techniques including estimation

Production
- Understanding written information regarding schedules, budgets, maps and scene requirements
- Interpreting technical manuals related to camera and computer usage

Post-production
- Creating written documents such as logs and paper edits to support editing process
- Listening to soundtrack information and responding with sound editing solutions

Distribution
- Speaking about their projects during promotional events
- Creating Press Kits with written documents
- Listening to audience feedback

Thinking Skills

SCANS	Filmmaking
Learners think creatively, make decisions, solve problems, visualize, know how to learn and reason.	*Students develop skills by:*

SCANS

Learners think creatively, make decisions, solve problems, visualize, know how to learn and reason.

Creative Thinking

Learners generate new ideas.

Decision Making

Learners specify goals and constraints, generate alternatives, consider risks, and evaluate and choose best alternative.

Problem Solving

Learners recognize problems and devise and implement plan of action.

Seeing Things in the Mind's Eye

Learners organize and process symbols, pictures, graphs, objects and other information.

Knowing How to Learn

Learners use efficient learning techniques to acquire and apply new knowledge and skills.

Reasoning

Learners discover a rule or principle underlying the relationship between two or more objects and apply it when solving a problem.

Filmmaking

Students develop skills by:

Development
- Brainstorming and using creative thinking to explore new ideas for film projects
- Acquiring knowledge during research and idea development
- Choosing best ideas to become the Script

Pre-production
- Organizing pictures and other information through storyboarding
- Specifying goals during scene breakdowns and planning
- Recognizing deficiencies and solving problems

Production
- Articulating goals in Call Sheets
- Solving problems during filming
- Evaluating progress and revising plans with Production Reports

Post-production
- Evaluating film footage
- Choosing best material for editing
- Understanding reasoning behind the use of different kinds of shots (wide, close, high angle, low angle, etc.)

Distribution
- Evaluation of filmmaking process
- Brainstorming of presentation ideas
- Organizing finished film and support material for web delivery and Press Kits

Personal Qualities

SCANS	Filmmaking
Learners display responsibility, self-esteem, sociability, self-management, integrity and honesty.	*Students develop skills by:*

<table>
<tr><td valign="top">

Responsibility
    Learners exert a high level of effort and persevere towards goal attainment.

Self-Esteem
    Learners believe in their own self-worth and maintain a positive view of self.

Sociability
    Learners demonstrate understanding, friendliness, adaptability, empathy, and politeness in group settings.

Self-Management
    Learners assess themselves accurately, set personal goals, monitor progress, and exhibit self-control.

Integrity/Honesty
    Learners choose ethical courses of action.

</td><td valign="top">

Development
- Demonstrating sociability in discussions regarding project
- Demonstrating empathy, friendliness, adaptability, understanding and politeness during brainstorming and script development sessions

Pre-production
- Setting well defined goals
- Paying attention to details
- Demonstrating knowledge of own skills and abilities during planning

Production
- Monitoring group and self progress
- Recognizing the impact of 'letting down the team'
- Demonstrating responsibility with equipment, time and resources
- Demonstrating responsibility for their part of the production

Post-production
- Demonstrating sociability during group editing decision-making processes

Distribution
- Evaluating self and team
- Exhibiting self-control and responding to feedback unemotionally
- Asserting themselves in interviews and public presentations of the project

</td></tr>
</table>

Workplace Competencies: Resources

SCANS	Filmmaking
Learners identify, organize, plan, and allocate resources.	*Students develop skills by:*

<table>
<tr><td>

Time

Learners select goal-relevant activities, rank them, allocate time, and prepare and follow schedules.

Money

Learners use or prepare budgets, make forecasts, keep records, and make adjustments to meet objectives.

Material and Facilities

Learners acquire, store, allocate, and use materials or space efficiently.

Human Resources

Learners assess skills and distribute work accordingly, evaluate performance and provide feedback.

</td><td>

Development
- Teams creating goal-relevant projects
- Distributing production roles and responsibilities through out filmmaking team

Pre-production
- Breaking down Scripts to identify the components of each scene
- Creating budgets that identify the resources that are required and the amount of time that has been allocated for filming each scene
- Creating, maintaining and adapting records of the many components relating to the project (Breakdown Sheets, Schedules, Budgets, Location Surveys)
- Acquiring, storing, allocating and efficiently using materials such as wardrobe, props and other production materials
- Forecasting what will happen and comparing it to what actually happens

Production
- Performing solo and group production responsibilities
- Monitoring and adjusting schedules
- Monitoring and adjusting budgets

Post-production
- Utilizing time management and planning to enhance successful editing

Distribution
- Evaluating of self and group's performance

</td></tr>
</table>

Workplace Competencies: Interpersonal

SCANS	Filmmaking
Learners work with others.	*Students develop skills by:*

SCANS	Filmmaking
Participate as Member of a Team Learners contribute to group effort. **Teach Others New Skills** Learners share skills with others. **Serve Clients/Customers** Learners work to satisfy customers' expectations. **Exercise Leadership** Learners communicate ideas to justify position, persuade and convince others, responsibly challenge existing procedures and policies. **Negotiate** Learners work toward agreements involving exchange of resources, resolve divergent interests. **Works with Diversity** Learners work well with men and women from diverse backgrounds.	**Development** • Working in teams to explore divergent and common interests to define the film project • Designing projects that exercise leadership by challenging existing policies and procedures in the community • Defining goals of 'client' or project • Communicating, discussing, negotiating divergent interests to produce a common Script. **Pre-production** • Working in teams to define objectives • Working in teams to solve problems • Taking on leadership roles in various filmmaking departments • Negotiating shooting schedules and shooting requirements **Production** • Working in teams to achieve goals during filming • Working with men and women from diverse backgrounds, and from outside the school **Post-production** • Negotiating editing decisions as a team **Distribution** • Evaluating team's success with the filmmaking process • Evaluating team's success at satisfying 'client' or project expectations • Exercising leadership in the community with public presentations

Workplace Competencies: Information ▪ ▪ ▪

SCANS	Filmmaking
Learners acquire and use information.	*Students develop skills by:*

SCANS — Learners acquire and use information.

Acquire and Evaluate Information

Organize and Maintain Information

Interpret and Communicate Information

Use Computers to Process Information

Filmmaking — Students develop skills by:

Development
- Acquiring and evaluating research information relating to the film idea being explored
- Interpreting and communicating information in script form

Pre-production
- Breaking down Scripts and entering details of required criteria into databases
- Organizing and maintaining databases of production information including crew and cast Contact Lists, Location Surveys and Scene Breakdowns
- Sorting information to produce Budgets and Schedules
- Maintaining databases related to the Shooting Schedule and Budget, and publishing updates

Production
- Acquiring and organizing production information and presenting reports as daily Call Sheet prior to production
- Presenting information regarding the results of each day's production in the form of a Production Report.

Post-production
- Evaluating information related to the editing process
- Organizing information as Edit Decision Lists on paper or on computer

Distribution
- Acquiring and evaluating the process and results of the filmmaking project
- Communicating information about the project to media around the community and school

Workplace Competencies: Systems

SCANS	Filmmaking
5. Learners understand complex inter-relationships.	**Students develop skills by:**

SCANS

5. Learners understand complex inter-relationships.

Understand Systems

Learners know how social, organizational, and technological systems work and operates effectively with them.

Monitor and Correct Performance

Learners distinguish trends, predict impacts on systems operations, diagnose deviations in systems' performance, and correct malfunctions.

Improve or Design Systems

Learners suggest modifications to existing systems and develop new or alternative systems to improve performance.

Filmmaking

Students develop skills by:

Development
- Investigating social, organization and technological systems as research and development of project ideas

Pre-production
- Analyzing and understanding organizational systems related to filmmaking
- Analyzing and understanding time management and project management systems

Production
- Monitoring and correction of filmmaking production systems through Call Sheets and Production Reports

Post-production
- Understanding of post-production process and investigation into new and alternate ideas to improve editing performance

Distribution
- Evaluating filmmaking process and suggesting modifications or alternative processes to improve filmmaking systems in the classroom or school

Workplace Competencies: Technology

SCANS	Filmmaking
5. *The student works with a variety of technologies.*	***Students develop skills by:***

<table>
<tr><td valign="top">

Select Technology

Learners choose procedures, tools or equipment, including computers and related technologies.

Apply Technology to Task

Learners understand overall intent and proper procedures for setup and operation of equipment.

Maintain and Troubleshoot Equipment

Learners prevent, identify, or solve problems with equipment, including computers and other technologies.

</td><td valign="top">

Development
- Working with various software to develop ideas
- Familiarization with Web research strategies
- Working with word processing programs to develop Scripts

Pre-production
- Working with word processing, spreadsheet and database software to break down Scripts, create Budgets, Schedules and other planning documents
- Working with visual media to create Story-boards

Production
- Working with digital video cameras
- Working with digital still cameras
- Working with audio recording equipment
- Working with lighting and camera moving equipment

Post-production
- Working with digital video editing software
- Working with image manipulation software
- Working with scanners
- Creating video dubs

Distribution
- Working with data projectors and video monitors
- Creating web sites
- Creating DVDs and CDs
- Creating Electronic Press Kits

</td></tr>
</table>

Part 4:

Teachers as Directors

"Finally, you know, I consider that my profession as a director is not exactly like a supervisor. No. We are simply, midwives. The actor has something inside himself but very often he doesn't realize what he has in mind, in his own heart, and you have to tell him. You have to help him find himself."
Jean Renoir

22: Teachers as Directors

What exactly do directors do? When you mention the word film director, what comes to mind?

Do you see a tyrannical figure marching around the set, megaphone in hand, yelling, "Action!" "Cut!" and, "One more time with feeling!" ?

Hollywood films about filmmaking have perpetuated this myth about how directors work. And although there are directors who do yell, and who do believe they are actually rulers of small independent countries, oblivious of their arrogance or their indifference for others, for the most part, directors, and particularly good directors, do not work this way.

Good directors don't direct; they observe.

They don't tell actors how to act; they help actors discover for themselves what real people do.

They don't say, "I think;" they say, "I wonder."

They don't arrive on the set with answers. They arrive with questions.

They investigate massive amounts of information about the story, characters, locations, design, style, theme and secrets that the screenplay holds and call it preparation.

Armed with this preparation and with these questions, they work with their actors and crew towards the discovery of truths. Truths about the story, about the characters, about people in general, and ultimately, truths about themselves. This is important to note because I want teachers to also be 'Directors in the Classroom,' working along with their students. I want them to give up the control that prevents discovery.

There must be a shift from the tyrannical film director

style of teaching. It cannot be about telling, memorizing and commanding.

Like Elia Kazan, John Cassavettes and other great directors, educators must switch from tellers to enablers. They must facilitate the discovery of information that will make the knowledge that is earned personal and meaningful. It is this understanding of the knowledge that makes performances and learning brilliant.

If I am working with an actor and they ask me, "What do you think my character would do in this situation?" I must resist from giving an answer, even though I may have my own ideas from my research. Instead, I would ask them, "What do you think your character would do in this situation?" If they're stuck, I would refine the exploration. "Do you know anyone who has ever been in a situation like your character?" or, "Have you ever been in a situation like this yourself?" I must be prepared to offer my own experiences. "Well, I had a friend who was in a situation like your character is in," or, "I was once in a situation like that…"

As a director, I must constantly be looking for ways to bounce questions, processes and revelations back into the actor's lap. I must listen for small discoveries that are whispered and suggested, and celebrate them with energy and excitement. I must encourage them to go further, to consider what they have learned, to ask more questions, and to investigate for themselves the various possibilities that lay ahead.

For students to have long term success with developing process skills, personal skills, and the understanding of knowledge, we must as educators incorporate these traits of great directors, of these facilitators of discovery.

Tyrant or Guide.

Which Director would you want to work with?

Which Director will you be?

Appendix

"The great films have not been made yet. The ones who will make them are out there, though, riding a skateboard."
Robert Altman

Appendix 1 • Glossary of Production Terms

A

Actor A person who brings to life a character from a script.

Adaptation A screenplay that is based on another work, for example, a novel, stage play, poem, song or short story.

ADR *See* **Automatic Dialogue Replacement**

Art Director The person responsible for producing the visual look of the film or video production. This may include the supervision of decisions related to locations, set design, hair, makeup, props, set dressings and sometimes lighting. This person usually reports to the Production Designer. *See* **Production Designer**

Assistant Director *See* **First Assistant Director**

Audio Track *See* **Soundtrack**

Automatic Dialogue Replacement (ADR) The process of replacing the original dialogue that was recorded with new dialogue. This is sometimes required if the original audio was not clearly recorded or the audio for whatever reason is unusable.

B

Best Boy The assistant to the Gaffer.

Boom A long pole with a microphone at one end that allows the sound mixer to place the microphone close to the action during filming. The Boom Operator operates the boom.

Breakdown An analysis of the script, scene by scene. It identifies and lists the cast, the locations, the sets, the props, wardrobe requirements, etc. Each department breaks down the script to identify exactly what specifics are required of their team.

Budget The detailed plan of what it will take (in terms of money) to produce the project. In a classroom, it is often a detailed plan of how much time has been allotted to the various phases of production.

C

Call Sheet A form that lists all the logistical requirements for a particular day's shoot. It is usually distributed to the cast and crew on the day prior to filming. It lists all the cast, sometimes all the crew, the location of the shoot, the start times, the scenes that will be filmed, and any special equipment, props, wardrobe, hair, makeup, special effects or any particular materials.

Camera Operator (also Cameraman) The person, man or woman, who follows the movement of the actors through the viewfinder of the camera, and who is responsible for the smooth and appropriate panning, tilting and framing of the image.

Casting Director The person responsible for making recommendations on the selection of actors for a production.

Character The people, animals, monsters or other creatures described in a screenplay.

Cinematographer *See* **Director of Photography**

Clapper Board *See* **Slate**

Contingency (fund) On production budgets, it is an allowance that is added to the budget to cover unforeseen expenses. It is usually 10%. On classroom budgets, it may be added to represent unforeseen delays.

Continuity Because most productions are shot out of sequence, each department ensures that action, wardrobe, lighting and other elements match from take to take and from scene to scene. The ultimate responsibility for the continuity of a film belongs to the script supervisor. *See also* **Script Supervisor**

Copyright The legal right of creative artists to control the use, reproduction and performance of all or portions of their original works. *See also* **Public Domain**

Craft Services The person or persons on a crew who ensure that there is a supply of coffee, juices and snacks available at all times on the set.

Crew The group of people who work together to create the production.

Dailies The footage from a particular day's shooting. Before there was video, filmmakers had to wait to see what their daily efforts produced. At the end of each shooting day, the film, which had been exposed, was taken to a film lab where it was developed and printed. The next day, the filmmakers would watch the previous day's footage and determine if they should proceed or if something had to be refilmed. Today, using video, this screening happens simultaneously or at any time after it has been recorded. Also referred to as *rushes*.

Daily Production Report *See* **Production Report**

Day-out-of-days A cross-plot calendar that reports on which date each resource is required during the entire production. It is most commonly used for actors, but can also be used for a set, a location, a prop, special equipment or any other production element.

Deal Memo A contractually binding document that summarizes the terms that the negotiating parties have agreed upon. Usually this is followed at a later date with a 'full and formal' agreement.

Deferral An arrangement whereby individuals or suppliers agree to wait for all or part of their fees until a later time. This is usually defined as after the production generates revenues.

Depth of Field The area between the nearest object in focus and the furthest object in focus.

Development The first phase in filmmaking where the script, budget, schedules, actors, directors and other creative personnel are investigated and acquired in order to get to the point of financing. In a classroom, it is determining the projects goals and guidelines, the filmmaking team, and the production of the Script.

Dialogue The words in the screenplay that the actors speak.

Director The person responsible for the overall creative vision of the project. They have input into the script, casting, production design and all other creative elements of the production. They are responsible for taking the words of the script and translating them into images and performances on the screen.

Director of Photography (DOP) The person who supervises the camera and lighting decisions on a production. The DOP works closely with the Director to determine the visual feel of the production and then work through the camera, lighting, and grip departments to manifest that vision. Sometimes referred to as the *cinematographer.*

Distributor The company or person who distributes, or who has the right to distribute, films and videos to markets. These markets include theatrical, non-theatrical, network television, home video, DVD, and the Internet.

Dolly A platform that the camera is placed on in order to produce a shot that incorporates movement of the camera. It can also be used as a verb, as in, "Let's dolly into the action."

DV Digital Video

E

Editor The individual responsible for assembling the separate takes and scenes that have been recorded to create the finished, coherent program.

Electronic Press Kits (EPK) Press Kits in the form of videotapes, CD-ROM, DVD or Web sites which contain video segments relating to the production. These can be interviews, behind the scenes footage, and sometimes footage from the finished program. *See also* **Press Kits**

F

Feature A full-length film, usually over ninety minutes in duration.

First Assistant Director (1ˢᵗ AD) The person who assists the director with the scheduling, the breakdown of the script, the shooting schedule and other aspects of organizing the production. On the set, the 1ˢᵗ AD manages the operation of the production and is responsible for ensuring that the scenes that have been selected for filming are ready for filming. They ask for, "Quiet on the set," they instruct the sound mixer to, "Roll sound," and they ask the camera assistant to, "Roll Camera." (The Director says, "Action.")

Focal Length The distance from a camera lens's focal point to its CCD imaging chips with the lens focus set to infinity. Wide angle views use short focal length; narrow field of view (telephoto) use longer focal lengths. Zoom lenses have a variable focal length.

Focus Puller Also referred to as the 1ˢᵗ Assistant Camera, this person ensures that the image that is recorded is always in sharp focus. The Focus Puller adjusts the focus ring on the camera while watching the performance unfold in front of the camera.

Foley The synchronizing of sound effects to images on screen. For example, the addition of the sound of footsteps to a scene where actors are walking, would be an example of Foley. It is usually performed by a Foley artist, who, while watching the image on screen, creates the desired sounds.

G

Gaffer The person who is the head of the lighting and electrical department for the production.

Grip A member of the film crew who is responsible for setting up lighting stands, laying dolly track, erecting scaffolding, and securing the camera to vehicles, ladders and other devices. *See also* **Key Grip**

K

Key Art The imagery used to identify a production for marketing purposes. The key art is used on posters, video covers, press kits and other advertising and promotional materials.

Key Grip The head of the grip department. *See also* **Grip**

L

License Fee A broadcaster's payment that gives them the right to broadcast a particular program for a specific number of occasions over a specified length of time.

Location Any site where filming will take place other than in a studio.

Location Manager The person responsible for finding, securing, negotiating for and administrating locations for a production.

Location Scout The person who assists the Location Manager in finding a location. This person make inquiries, take photographs, and presents their findings to the Location Manager.

Looping   The recording of dialogue to replace unusable or non-existent audio. *See also* **Automatic Dialogue Replacement (ADR)**

M

Mixing   The synthesis of the dialogue, music and sound effects tracks to produce a single, balanced sound track in such a way that the appropriate sound is heard, at an appropriate volume level, at each point in the program.

Music and effects track (M/E Track)   The portion of the soundtrack that contains only the music and the sound effects. This is requested when a distributor is dubbing the film into another language. Also called an *international track*.

Music Cue Sheet   A list of all the music that is used in a production that includes each piece's length, composer, publisher, affiliation and usage (background or feature).

P

Pan   When used in reference to camera movement, it is the horizontal sweeping movement of a camera across a scene.

Pitching   The oral presentation of the project to prospective supporters.

Post-production   The phase of filmmaking that begins after Principal Photography is completed. This includes the editing, sound, music, mixing and final finishing that leads to the completion of a finished program.

Pre-production (prep)   The phase of filmmaking that begins after Development. This includes all the scheduling, breakdowns, location managing, casting, and other preparations required for filming. Pre-production ends the day before shooting begins.

Press Kit   Marketing materials that have been combined into one package for distribution to newspapers, magazines and other members of the press. The kits usually contain photographs, biographies, plot synopsis, producer, director and screenwriter notes. *See also* **Electronic Press Kits (EPK)**

Principal Photography   The recording of all scenes that require the main body of the crew and any of the leading performers. Sometimes referred to as *Production*.

Producer The person with the overall responsibility for the production. The produceris responsible for, and has the ultimate control over, spending, hiring, scheduling, and selection of all elements in a production. His or her duties may be shared with associate producers, line producers, co-producers and executive producers.

Production The phase of filmmaking that begins on the first day of shooting and continues until all filming had been completed. Sometimes referred to as *Principal Photography*.

Production Coordinator The person who is responsible for communicating information to all who are involved in a production. This information includes script changes, schedules and scheduling changes, travel and accommodation information, and any other information that is required to keep personnel informed and aligned.

Production Designer The individual who works with the director to create the overall look, mood and style of the production. This person is the head of the Art Department who supervises and coordinates the efforts of the Art Director, Set Designers, Wardrobe, Hair, and Makeup personnel as well as others in the department.

Production Manager (PM) The person who supervises the overall logistical arrangements for a production. Usually reports directly to the producer.

Production Notes The detailed documentation of the making of the production, as prepared by the Unit Publicist.

Production Report A detailed form that reports on each day's shooting activity. It lists exactly what scenes were recorded, who was involved, what time everyone started and ended, and any details particular to that shooting day. It is completed by the assistant director after production has ended each day and delivered to the production manager who, after authorizing it, delivers it to the producer.

Production Stills Photographs taken during the creation of the project, usually by the Set (or Unit) Photographer. These are then used to market and publicize the film.

Property Manager The person in charge of all the props.

Props Movable items that are handled by the actors. For example, on a kitchen set, the props may include a bread knife, a piece of toast, a newspaper, a pair of eyeglasses, a jar of honey, a wallet or a cup of hot coffee.

Public Domain Creative works such as songs, films or books that are unprotected by copyright, usually because the copyright has expired. *See also* **Copyright**

Publicist The person on a production crew who assembles and presents information about the production in such a way that favorable media attention is generated. This information includes production notes, photographs, biographies and video segments.

R

Rule of Thirds This is the basic principle that is the most valuable to a new photographer. This rule takes our rectangular shape and divides it into thirds. The key elements or objects in a composition should fall on one of these thirds lines. The one point on our photograph where the viewers' eye comes to rest should fall on one of these lines where both a horizontal and a vertical line come to rest.

Rushes *See* **Dailies**

S

Scene A sequence of events that moves the story forward and reveals characters. It can be any length, from a single line to multiple pages, but usually always takes place in a single location over a single period of time. Scenes combine to form acts, and the acts combine to form the screenplay.

Screenplay The script written for the film.

Screenwriter The person who writes the story, setting and characters that become the screenplay.

Script The written document that contains the actions, dialogue and descriptions of the story to be filmed.

Script Supervisor The person on the set who is ultimately responsible for ensuring that actions and elements of the film (like wardrobe, hair and props) match from take-to-take and scene-to-scene. Also records detailed information about each take and records the Director's choice of takes.

Second Unit A smaller sized crew that shoots additional footage for the production. This additional footage includes establishing shots, landscapes, exteriors of building, cars driving down roads and other shots or sequences that do not require dialogue.

Set In a script and script breakdown, it refers to where the action of a scene takes place. For example, a kitchen, a hospital room, a football field, or a waterfall. It can also refer to where the filming is taking place, as in, "Take this package to set."

Set Decorator The person who places objects and furniture in a room or building or outdoor location to make it look realistic. Attempts to match the set to the descriptions in the script.

Set Photographer The person who takes photographs on the set.

Shooting Script The final version of the script.

Short A film or video that runs less than thirty minutes.

Shot One continuous piece of recorded footage.

Shot List A list of all the shots required on a scene-by-scene, day-to-day or location-by-location basis. This list is created by the director in collaboration with the director of photography, 1st AD, and other personnel.

Slate A board that identifies the take, scene, date and film production. A clapperboard is a slate that has a hinged arm that produces a 'clap' when lowered quickly. In film post-production, the sound of the 'clap' and the image of the arm and board meeting provide a reference point for the editors to sync up the audio and video tracks of each shot.

Sound Mixer The person responsible for recording the dialogue and sound during production. Monitors the volume level of the audio signals that are being recorded.

Soundtrack The portion of the video tape or film that contains the audio information of the production. The soundtrack is made up of the dialogue, music and sound effect tracks.

Special Effects Supervisor The person on the crew is responsible for the special effects, including car chases, fires, breaking glass, etc.

Stand-in An actor or individual who substitutes for the main actor when the director or camera team is designing a shot.

Storyboard A tool for communicating how the film will look like. It is a visual document, resembling a comic book, which portrays the design and sequence of the shots that will make up the film.

Stunt Coordinator The person on the crew responsible for the safe execution of falls, fights, car chases and other potentially hazardous actions.

T

Take In production, it refers to a single recorded performance. A scene may be rerecorded many times in an attempt to record a flawless performance. Each attempt is referred to as a take.

Tilt When used in reference to camera movement, it is the vertical sweeping movement of a camera across a scene.

Trailer A short promotional program that advertises another longer production. Trailers are commonly seen in theatres or on videos before the main attraction.

Treatment A narrative synopsis of a screenplay. It includes the descriptions of the characters, the plot that they are involved in and often some examples of sample dialogue.

U

Unit Publicist *See* **Publicist**

V

Video A medium for recording images and audio synchronously.

Weather Cover Also referred to as *cover set*.

White Balance Adjusting a camera's light filtering system to ensure that the camera accurately records true colors. Different lighting conditions affect how cameras record colors.

Wrap The end of shooting. "That's a wrap," can signify the completion of filming of a given day, a given location, or of the entire production.

Z

Zoom On a camera, to change the focal length to/from wide-angle and telephoto.

(Courtesy of Digital Origin and Media 100: www. digitalmedia.com)

3-point edit Marking three of the four points needed to place a source clip into a program and allowing the editing software to calculate the fourth point. For example, an editor identifies an In and Out point in the source clip and an In point in the program and allows the editing software to calculate the Out point in the program. This technique allows for complex multi-track synchronized video/audio editing.

4-point edit Marking all four points to place a source clip into a program. The speed of the source clip is adjusted (speeded up or slowed down) to fit the space allowed for it in the program.

A

A/B Roll Editing Editing is performed using two video sources, A & B, and a video switcher or mixer that allows for a variety of transitions between them as they are output to a video recorder.

action safe area Determines where movement or visual detail is the least likely to get cropped. See also **safe area, title safe area** and **overscan**.

alpha channel Information attached to each pixel that represents how that pixel is to be blended with background.

analog media The term used to refer to the media found on traditional videotape recordings.

animation Any change of a parameter over time. Generally refers to a change in position of the video frame, moving the video over a background while it plays.

anti-aliasing The process of smoothing the edges of graphics and text to prevent flicker and jagged edges.

aspect ratio Proportional height and width of a video image. The NTSC standard for is 4:3 for conventional monitors such as home television sets, and 16:9 for HDTV.

assemble edit Method for building a videotape in which a series of clips are placed one after the other to create or assemble a program.

audio dub Recording audio over an existing video program without affecting the video images.

AVI Audio-Video Interleave, which is a video format for Windows.

B

back-timing Using a 3-point edit to mark two Out points and one In point, allowing the computer to match up the two Out points and calculate the remaining In point. For example, marking an In and Out point on a source clip and an Out point of a program and allowing the editing software to calculate the In point of the program.

band wipe Transition that produces the effect of displaying an incoming clip as alternating bands that eventually cover the outgoing clip.

barn door wipe A transition that opens or closes the first frame of an incoming clip over the outgoing clip as if it were two sliding doors.

bin A location for storing and organizing clips.

C

character generator (CG) The equipment used in a linear editing suite to create titles or other text on video.

chrominance Portion of video signal that carries hue and saturation color information. Also see luminance.

chroma key filter A filter that allows for a selected color in a clip to be made transparent. It is generally used to superimpose one clip on another.

clip A set of contiguous frames beginning at a designated In point and ending at a designated Out point.

codec Component of a video system that encodes video data into its compressed format, and decodes data from its compressed format. Video data is stored in a compressed format. When an effect is applied to one or more tracks of video, the video must be uncompressed in order to compute (render) the effect. Historically, codecs have been implemented on specialized hardware. Software codecs are now more prominent because desktop computers are now fast enough to support video processing.

color palette Software user interface for choosing a desired color for use with many of the filters and transitions. A color might be chosen to be replaced, to be keyed out, to be changed, etc.

component Video signal that keeps luminance and chrominance separate for better picture quality.

composite Video signal that combines luminance and chrominance in a single signal. Less expensive than component video, but lower picture quality.

compression The digital representation of media in an efficient storage format. For video, motion-JPEG is often used. Compression may be lost in that the original picture cannot be reconstructed exactly.

color adjust filter An editing software filter that produces a change in the color aspects of a clip by allowing adjustment of individual channels.

cross fade audio transition A transition that causes the end of one audio clip to fade out, while the beginning of the next clip fades in.

cut An abrupt transition between two clips. The first frame of the incoming clip immediately follows the last frame of the outgoing clip.

cutaway Transitional footage normally inserted between cuts containing the same subject in slightly different screen positions to avoid a 'jump cut'.

cut point The position of a cut relative to an overlying transition.

D

device control software A software module that controls a video deck to allow the capture of source clips to the hard drive of a computer.

Digital 8 Sony's proprietary digital camcorder format, which records digital video onto standard 8mm and Hi8 tapes.

digitize To convert an analog video or audio signal into a digital signal that can be used by a computer.

dissolve transition A transition in which the end of one clip gradually blends with the beginning of the next.

dropout Videotape signal 'voids,' which are visible as white specks or streaks. Normally the result of tiny bare spots on a tape's magnetic particle coating, or tape debris covering particles and blocking signals.

drop frame timecode Timecode that is accurate relative to actual video running time. The numerical reference drops two numbers every minute to allow for the fact that there are actually 29.97 frames of video per second, rather than 30 frames per second.

drop shadow A shadow that is offset from an object or text in a video.

E

EDL Edit Decision List. A computer generated list containing information about a specific program, the **SMPTE** timecodes and options chosen during production. It is used to inform an editing system of all the parameters involved in the creation of that program. An EDL is generally used to assemble a program in a traditional video editing suite.

erase A procedure for removing media from a video program, leaving black space (called filler) in its place to maintain the spacing and length of the entire program. Sometimes called a *non-ripple edit*.

fade filter The filter that raises or lowers video levels in clips. With the Fade filter a clip will change over time to all one color or black (fade out); or will gradually develop from a color or black (fade in).

field Half of a video frame, either the even or odd scan lines.

filler Blank space added to the Timeline in the course of editing a program.

filter A computer software module used to process and modify digital video for adding special effects to a program.

force an edit To insert a cut at a desired point in a clip.

frame One complete still image of video media. Video media is made up of a series of frames. Each video frame has two interlaced fields.

full field A complete video image consisting of two fields of video per frame.

FX track A separate track on the Timeline used strictly for creating special video effects.

G

generation Original recorded footage is called 'first-generation.' A copy of the original is second-generation video. A copy of a copy is called third generation, and so forth.

H

headroom Space between the top of the subject and a monitor's upper screen edge. Leaving space for 'headroom' is common practice.

hold An interpolation setting that maintains settings from one key frame until the next key frame and uses the space of only one frame to jump to the next setting.

I

identifier Name or number given to a clip or segment of a video to allow for easy recognition of the segment and its contents.

image resolution A measurement of the quality of a video image based on the number of pixels that make up the image.

In point The SMPTE time code of the specific frame at which a clip begins.

insert edit   Placing a section of a source clip in the Timeline at the position of the Timeline cursor. The media currently to the right of the insertion point is moved farther to the right to accommodate the insertion of the new clip.

interesting time A place in a video program where an editorial event occurs, such as the beginning of a filter or transition, new clip, or key frame.

interpolation The progressive calculation of a parameter between key frames.

iris transition A transition that creates the appearance of an enlarging opening revealing a incoming clip underneath. It is made to look like the iris of the eye opening, or enlarging.

J

jog To move forward or backward in video or audio media by playing at slow speed through it.

JPEG (Joint Photographic Experts Group) An international standard for still picture data compression.

jump cut An instantaneous transition between two scenes that have identical subjects in slightly different screen locations, which makes the subject appear to jump within the screen. A cutaway shot remedies the distracting jump appearance.

kerning The amount of space between text characters. Kerning varies between fonts.

keyframe A frame at which a set of specific parameters is assigned. For example, a title can be instructed to move between different coordinates on the screen, each coordinate is associated with a specified keyframe.

key out Removing a section of video by making it transparent by creating an alpha channel based on color. (Chroma Key) or on brightness (Luma Key).

L

leading The space between lines of text.

linear Movement between key frame settings along straight lines.

linear editing The traditional form of tape based video editing.

log The numbers, either SMPTE or computer generated (for video that doesn't contain SMPTE timecodes), that editing softward uses to identify media. The log also includes additional information, such as tape identifiers and clip duration.

luminance Black and white portion of a video signal representing picture contrast and brightness.

M

mirror filter Filter that flips frames horizontally to create an opposite but identical image.

N

non-drop frame timecode Timecode that does not compensate for the 29.97 frames of video per second of NTSC video, rather than 30 frames per second. Each frame is assigned a unique, consecutive SMPTE time code.

NTSC The National Television Standards Committee.

NTSC signal The standard composite video signal adopted by the NTSC that has 525 interlaced lines at a frame rate of 29.97 frames per second.

O

off line When no disk file exists for a reference to a clip in a program, the file is said to be off line.

on disk The media file for a clip is stored on a hard drive and referenced from within a program.

opacity The degree to which an image is transparent, allowing images behind to visually show through.

Out point The SMPTE time code defining the end of a clip. The frame with this time code is not included in the clip.

overscan The CCDs in digital cameras actually scan a picture that is bigger than the displayable view size of a standard television. Overscan is used to make sure that even when the TV device is not properly trimmed there are no black borders. This is occasionally necessary because some televisions generate a video pattern that is smaller than the visible screen area, resulting in an image that is smaller (and less legible) than it needs to be. The video quality of pixels at the extreme edges of the overscan area may not be reliable and when played back on the camera LCD display overwrite edit.

P

PAL Phase Alternating Line.
PAL signal The most common composite video signal used in Europe. It has a frame rate of 25 frames per second.

pan setting When used in reference to audio, the setting that determines how audio output is divided between left and right speakers.

pixel A single picture element. The smallest element in a graphic image. Pixels are combined with other pixels to make up a graphic image. Picture quality increases as the number of pixels increase in a measured area of an image.

point A standard measurement unit for type sizes. One point equals approximately 1/72 of an inch.

primary source clip A source clip that has media attached to it. The original source clip from which secondary source clips and reference clips are created.

program A sequence of reference clips arranged in a meaningful order. The final result of production with a video program.

project Organizational unit containing the media units that when incorporated and edited will constitute a program.

project preset Options that define the parameters for the production of a program, such as audio sampling rate, that are established before beginning production.

Q

QuickTime™ System software from Apple Computer, Inc. that enables the storage, editing, and playing of digitized video and audio media on a computer.

R

radial wipe transition A transition that sweeps away the outgoing clip with a circular or semi-circular motion to reveal the incoming clip.

render The processing of a series of individual clips, transitions and filters into a single playable track.

roll edit An editing process where both outgoing and incoming clips are trimmed at a cut point to shorten one while lengthening the other to maintain the overall length of a program.

S

safe areas Regions of the screen that won't get cropped when shown on different television monitors

scroll Moving text from the bottom to top and continuing off the visual boundaries.

scrub To play through an audio or video clip interactively (under manual control) to evaluate it or locate a specific event.

secondary source clip A source clip created from a primary source clip, a subclip. It contains no media, it only refers to the primary clip.

shuttle To move smoothly, forward or backward, through video or audio media at a constant rate.

SMPTE Abbreviation for the Society of Motion Picture and Television Engineers.
SMPTE timecode The timecode used by the SMPTE to identify frames in a videotape. Each frame has a unique address in an hours:minutes:seconds:frames format.

source clip A clip that refers directly to physical media.

splice The physical act of cutting a medium, such as film or audio tape, to add new tape to it or take out portions of it.

spline A setting that produces movement between key frame settings along curved lines; creating a smooth, flowing motion. split edit (L-cut or J-cut). Adjusting synchronized audio or video clips so that one starts slightly before or after the other.

step To move forward or backward one frame at a time.

stereo Audio split on two physical tracks, one on the right and one on the left.

T

timeline The graphic representation of a programs duration.

title safe area Central region of the screen where text will generally be most readable. See also action safe, safe areas and overscan.

track A horizontal band that graphically represents a series of clips in your program. The window usually has multiple tracks containing different types of media.

transition The change from one clip to another in a video program.

trim handles Extra frames before and after the In and Out points for a source clip to allow for trimming and transitions.

V

venetian blind wipe A transition that produces the effect of having an outgoing clip displayed in strips over the incoming clip. The strips open, like a Venetian blind, to reveal the incoming clip.

W

wipe A type of transition that uses a moving edge to replace the current clip to reveal the next clip.

Z

zoom In post-production, an editing filter that simulates the effect of having a camera move in very close to the subject, objects, or areas in a frame; or move away from the subject and display a wide view of the entire frame.

The following forms and checklists may be photocopied and distributed in classrooms. As well, you will find the same forms in 8 1/2 x 11 inch format as PDF files on the enclosed CD.

Please check our web site:

<www.thedirectorintheclassroom.com>

for updated forms, checklists and additional resources.

Important Note:

The permission/release forms included in the following Appendix are meant to be examples only and not meant to take the place of legal forms authorized by your school board. Please check with your school regarding policies, insurance, liability and procedures related to video production.

The Director in the Classroom • Filmmaker's Checklist

Development
- ❏ Brainstorm and research ideas
- ❏ Pitch ideas and project
- ❏ Write Script

Pre-production
- ❏ Create Storyboard
- ❏ Survey and select location(s)
- ❏ Create Scene Breakdowns
- ❏ Create Shooting Schedule and Budget

Production
- ❏ Create Shot List
- ❏ Obtain equipment
- ❏ Film required scenes
- ❏ Log footage
- ❏ Return equipment
- ❏ Create Production Report

Post-production
- ❏ Review footage
- ❏ Create paper edit
- ❏ Import footage into computer and edit picture, transitions, sound, titles and credits
- ❏ Export for viewing

Distribution
- ❏ Present finished film to class
- ❏ Organize additional screenings
- ❏ Produce publicity material

CD Filename: filmmaker.pdf

The Director in the Classroom • Team Filmmakers' Checklist

Development

Writer	❑ Writes Script
Director	❑ Leads brainstorming
Camera	❑ Researches visual imagery
Editor	❑ Leads research
Producer	❑ Pitches project

Pre-production

Writer	❑ Creates Scene Breakdown
Director	❑ Creates Storyboards
Camera	❑ Creates Shooting Schedule
Editor	❑ Creates Equipment and Contact Lists
Producer	❑ Creates Budgets

Production

Writer	❑ Records sound
Director	❑ Determines what to shoot
Camera	❑ Operates the camera
Editor	❑ Logs field footage
Producer	❑ Creates Production Reports

Post-production

Writer	❑ Writes narration if required
Director	❑ Finds additional sounds and music
Camera	❑ Finds additional photos and video
Editor	❑ Operates editing system and determines final edit decisions
Producer	❑ Schedules editing equipment and assists team with editing and organizes test screenings

Distribution

Writer	❑ Writes Press Kit information
Director	❑ Organizes interviews
Camera	❑ Creates stills from videotape
Editor	❑ Produces promotional 'trailers'
Producer	❑ Organizes screenings

CD Filename: filmmaker5.pdf

The Director in the Classroom • Producing Department Team Tasks

Development
- ❑ Assists executive producer in organizing departments
- ❑ Helps develop project ideas
- ❑ Creates framework for brainstorming
- ❑ Works with writing department to ensure screenplay is completed
- ❑ Delivers screenplay to executive producer

Pre-production
- ❑ Creates and distributes Cast and Crew List
- ❑ Collates department budgets and produces and distributes master Budget
- ❑ Collates department schedules and produces and distributes Shooting Schedule
- ❑ Ensures each department has the equipment and supplies they require
- ❑ Ensures that students acting in the film have signed permission slips

Production
- ❑ Ensures Call Sheets are produced and distributed
- ❑ Ensures transportation to location has been organized
- ❑ Ensures all production equipment and materials are present on the set
- ❑ Monitors production and assists in problem-solving
- ❑ Meets with executive producer and presents updates on schedules and budgets
- ❑ Produces and distributes Production Reports at end of each day's shooting

Post-production
- ❑ Ensures editing department has all audio and video materials required
- ❑ Ensures copyrighted material has been cleared (music, video, photos)
- ❑ Ensures all borrowed equipment has been returned
- ❑ Organizes test screenings and records audience feedback
- ❑ Delivers final film to executive producer

Distribution
- ❑ Ensures that screenings occur in school and elsewhere
- ❑ Ensures that film is submitted to film festivals
- ❑ Ensures publicity department has necessary materials to promote the film

CD Filename: producing.pdf

The Director in the Classroom • The Director Team Tasks

Development
- ❑ Participates in brainstorming and developing ideas
- ❑ Researches content material related to the project
- ❑ Researches visual and audio ideas for the project
- ❑ Works with writing department to complete Script

Pre-production
- ❑ Supervises Storyboards
- ❑ Studies Script and becomes familiar with its goals, ideas and themes
- ❑ Meets with all departments to discuss production requirements
- ❑ Meets with producer to discuss schedules and budgets
- ❑ Rehearses actors

Production
- ❑ Prepares Shot Lists for each scene
- ❑ Works with Camera Department to set up each shot
- ❑ Ensures visual elements (sets, wardrobe, props, etc.) are as required
- ❑ Directs actors on set
- ❑ Determines when a shot has been performed competently
- ❑ Records the preferred shots for editing

Post-production
- ❑ Works with editing department to determine how to best tell the story with the audio and video materials available
- ❑ Works with editing department to find or produce additional material as required
- ❑ Attends test screenings and provides input for revisions
- ❑ Works with editing department to complete final version

Distribution
- ❑ Meets with media and provides interviews

CD Filename: director.pdf

The Director in the Classroom • Writing Department Team Tasks

Development
- ❑ Brainstorm and develop ideas
- ❑ Research content material related to the project
- ❑ Research visual and audio ideas for the project
- ❑ Work with director and producer to complete the Script

Pre-production
- ❑ Continue rewriting the Script as required
- ❑ Assist director in creating Storyboards

Production
- ❑ Assist director in preparing Shot Lists for each scene
- ❑ Consult with director as to which shots may be best for editing, and record that information
- ❑ Assist in improvising dialogue or rewriting scenes on location

Post-production
- ❑ Work with editing department to determine how to best tell the story with the audio and video materials available
- ❑ Works with editing department to find or produce additional material as required
- ❑ Write narration if required
- ❑ Attend test screenings and provide input for revisions

Distribution
- ❑ Write Press Kit information

CD Filename: writing.pdf

The Director in the Classroom • Locations Department Team Tasks

Development
- ❑ Research other videos, films and works of art for ideas on the use of location to enhance the film's ideas, goals and themes

Pre-production
- ❑ Create location breakdowns to determine what sets are required
- ❑ List possible locations for each set
- ❑ Scout possible locations and complete location survey for each location
- ❑ Photograph or videotape each location
- ❑ Present locations to team with recommendations
- ❑ Secure locations
- ❑ Create department Schedule and Budget

Production
- ❑ Create list of locations and when they will be required
- ❑ Communicate with location contact to inform and schedule arrival
- ❑ Coordinate arrival and departure

Post-production
- ❑ Ensure that location was left clean and orderly
- ❑ Send thank you cards to the location contact

Distribution
- ❑ Invite location contact person to a screening

CD Filename: locations.pdf

The Director in the Classroom • Art Department Team Tasks

Development
- ❑ Brainstorm visual ideas
- ❑ Research visual ideas
- ❑ Provide visual aids for pitching ideas and project

Pre-production
- ❑ Create breakdowns of visual requirements
- ❑ Create art department Schedule and Budget
- ❑ Design, create or source sets, costumes, props, dressing, hair and make-up

Production
- ❑ Assemble sets and provide set dressings and props
- ❑ Costume actors and provide hair and make-up where necessary
- ❑ Source last-minute ideas

Post-production
- ❑ Return borrowed items with thank you cards
- ❑ Store created materials in classroom studio

Distribution
- ❑ Create visual materials for Press Kits
- ❑ Create posters for screenings

CD Filename: art.pdf

The Director in the Classroom • Camera Department Team Tasks

Development
- ❑ Research visual imagery from works of art and other videos and movies

Pre-production
- ❑ Determine what camera equipment is required and sources that equipment
- ❑ Test camera equipment prior to filming and familiarize themselves with all aspects of the camera package
- ❑ Discuss lighting ideas with lighting department
- ❑ Discuss camera movement ideas with grip department
- ❑ Create department Schedule and Budget

Production
- ❑ Bring all required camera equipment to set
- ❑ Set up camera, sets white balance for the lighting being used, test records
- ❑ Mark slate to identify which take and which scene is being recorded
- ❑ Move camera smoothly during pans and tilts. Ensures focus.
- ❑ Ensure there is enough video tape in camera before each take
- ❑ Indicate to the sound department when the boom microphone is in frame
- ❑ Advise director if video recording is out of focus, or not properly executed and suggest methods to improve the recording on the next take
- ❑ Create Field Footage Reports that clearly identify what was shot
- ❑ At end of day, carefully store and return camera package

Post-production
- ❑ Liaise with editors to identify all recorded footage
- ❑ Re-shoot missing scenes or images if required
- ❑ Research additional video material (stock video footage)
- ❑ Send thank you cards for borrowed equipment

Distribution
- ❑ Videotape interviews for Electronic Press Kits

CD Filename: camera.pdf

The Director in the Classroom • Sound Department Team Tasks

Development
❑ Develop and research ideas related to sound design from other videos, movies and audio works

Pre-production
❑ Determine what kind of sound recording will be required
❑ Determine what kinds of microphones will be required
❑ Source microphones
❑ Assess location's suitability in terms of existing noise and traffic
❑ Create department Schedules and Budgets

Production
❑ Arrange and pick up audio equipment
❑ Link the external microphones to the camera
❑ Establish the best location of microphones for each shot
❑ Use boom poles to place microphones close to actors
❑ Monitor dialogue through headsets
❑ Advise director if audio recording is unclear and suggest methods to improve the audio recording on the next take
❑ Record ambient sound on each set (room tone)
❑ Provide audio reports, detailing what audio was recorded

Post-production
❑ Record additional sounds as required
❑ Re-record dialogue if required
❑ Records musicians and bands for music score if required
❑ Work with sound editor to ensure efficient locating of audio recording

Distribution
❑ Record interviews for publicity materials

CD Filename: sound.pdf

The Director in the Classroom • Dolly & Grip Department Team Tasks

Development

- ❑ Research ideas related to lighting from other videos, movies and works of art

Pre-production

- ❑ Assess locations for lighting obstacles and opportunities
- ❑ Assess locations for camera movement obstacles and opportunities
- ❑ Determine what kind of lighting and grip equipment will be required
- ❑ Source or create lighting and grip equipment
- ❑ Consult with the director and director of photography regarding lighting ideas
- ❑ Consult Storyboards for lighting objectives
- ❑ Consult Storyboards for camera movement objectives
- ❑ Create department Schedule and Budgets

Production

- ❑ Safely set up light stands and lights
- ❑ Safely lay extension cords and cables from lights to power outlets
- ❑ Arrange lights as per lighting plan
- ❑ Monitor the effect of light on the set
- ❑ Consult with director of photography to fine-tune lighting effects.
- ❑ Move camera smoothly (using wheelchairs, tracks, swivel chairs, etc.)
- ❑ Allow lights to cool, then disassemble them for storage and handling

Post-production

- ❑ Provide grip and lighting for any additional videotaping

Distribution

- ❑ Provide grip and lighting for videotaping any press-related interviews

CD Filename: dollygrip.pdf

The Director in the Classroom • Editing Department Team Tasks

Development
- ❑ Research ideas related to editing styles

Pre-production
- ❑ Consult Storyboards and become familiar with the editing intent of the production
- ❑ Make a list of audio, video and photographic materials required for editing separate from what is being recorded (for example: stock footage, music, sound effects)
- ❑ Create department Schedule and Budget

Production
- ❑ Find or produce the additional materials required for editing
- ❑ Work with sound department to record additional sounds required for editing
- ❑ Work with camera department to record additional video where required

Post-production
- ❑ Ensure footage logs exist of all materials
- ❑ Create paper edit
- ❑ Import camera footage into editing system
- ❑ Assemble rough cut
- ❑ Create picture cut with visual transitions and titles
- ❑ Add soundtracks containing music, sound effects or narration
- ❑ Export project for test screening
- ❑ Produce final edited version
- ❑ Export project for distribution

Distribution
- ❑ Work with unit publicist to create Electronic Press Kits

CD Filename: editing.pdf

The Director in the Classroom • Publicity Department Team Tasks

Development
- [ ] Research ideas related to publicizing the final video

Pre-production
- [ ] Design press kits and determine what materials should be collected during production
- [ ] Photograph and videotape 'behind the scenes' of the different departments at work
- [ ] Plan when and how publicity interviews will occur
- [ ] Create department Schedule and Budget

Production
- [ ] Photograph and videotape the crew at work on the set
- [ ] Photograph and videotape 'behind the scenes' work of the departments
- [ ] Conduct interviews with all personnel
- [ ] Contact local newspapers and media (if desired) to photograph and interview student filmmakers

Post-production
- [ ] Conduct additional interviews
- [ ] Photograph and videotape editing department at work
- [ ] Pull together visual and text elements for Press Kits

Distribution
- [ ] Coordinate local media to attend screenings (if desired)
- [ ] Arrange interviews between student filmmakers and media
- [ ] Organize and ship Press Kits
- [ ] Provide press material for submission to film festivals

CD Filename: publicity.pdf

The Director in the Classroom • Project Criteria

Date:_____

Purpose:

Subject*:*

Audience:

Venue:

Project Duration:

Deadline:

Delivery Format:

Mini DV	VHS	CD	DVD	Web	Email
☐	☐	☐	☐	☐	☐

Other:

Special Instructions:

CD Filename: criteria.pdf

Date:_____

Page _____ of _____

_____   _____

        Project Title   Executive Producer

Position	Name and Address	Telephone /Email

Pre–Production

CD Filename: contactlist.pdf

The Director in the Classroom • Location Survey

Set Name: _____

Location: _____

Contact Person #1: _____

Phone #: _____

Phone #: _____

Contact Person #2: _____

Phone #: _____

Phone #: _____

Location Lighting:

What kind of natural light exists?

Skylights_____ Windows_____

Doors_____ Candlelight_____

Mirrors_____

What kind of artificial lights:

Fluorescent _____ Tungsten _____

Halogen_____

Is power available at Location? _____

Outlets: 2 prong: ____ 3 prong__

Is there enough light,
or do you need more?

Lighting Notes:

Directions:

Parking:

Hours Available:_____

Washrooms: _____

Phone Location: _____

Equipment Access:

_____

Location Camera

Is there room to work?
to move the camera?
Where will the camera be pointing?

Camera notes:

Location Sound:

Is it quiet or noisy?
Is there traffic? Music? Machinery?

Sound Notes:

*Use back of form for directions,
maps and floorplans.*

CD Filename: locationsurvey.pdf

PERMISSION TO USE A LOCATION

I, _____give permission
to_____ to use my (our)
home, building, office, property or other area to be used as a location for the
student video production titled:

_____

The property to be used is located at:

_____

The student production shall be allowed access to the property at the following
dates and time:

_____

    Access is granted for the purpose of recording scenes (interior and/or exterior)
for a motion picture, and for bringing onto the property personnel and equipment
(including props and temporary sets) that may be necessary for this production.

    I also understand that this production may be broadcast or distributed at
the student producers' discretion, and may be seen on video, in theatres or on
broadcast television and other media.

    The producer agrees to remove all materials and equipment that were brought
in for the production, and to leave the location in as good as condition as when
they found it.

If required, the credit line shall read as follows:

_____

Signed _____

At_____

In the presence of:

_____
Location Owner or Manager

_____
Student Producer

Pre–Production

CD Filename: locationrelease.pdf

The Director in the Classroom • Budget

Date: _____   Project Title: _____

Executive Producer: _____

Pre-Production	When	Budget	Total Hours	
➢ Script ➢ Storyboard ➢ Planning				
Total				

Production	When	Budget	Total Hours	
Scene #	Total			

Post-Production	When	Budget	Total Hours	
➢ Log ➢ Editing ➢ Export ➢ Test Screening				
Total				

CD Filename: budget.pdf   **TOTAL**

Title: _____

The Director in the Classroom • Scene Breakdown Sheet

Date: _____

Project Title/No. _____

Executive Producer _____

Breakdown Page No. _____

Scene No. _____

Scene Name _____

Int. or Ext. _____

Description _____

Day or Night _____

Page Count _____

Cast	Stunts	Extras/Atmosphere
	Extras/Silent Bits	
Special Effects	Props	Vehicles/Animals
Wardrobe	Make-up/Hair	Sound Effects/Music
Special Equipment	Production Notes	

CD Filename: scene.pdf

The Director in the Classroom • Shooting Schedule

Date:

Project Title:

Day:

Scene#	Scene Description	Time Required

Day:

Scene#	Scene Description	Time Required

CD Filename: schedule.pdf

The Director in the Classroom • Production Checklist

	Out	In
CAMERA		
Camera		
Tripod		
Blank tapes (extras as well)		
Batteries (extras as well)		
AC power supply for camera		
LIGHTING		
Light kit		
Power cables		
Clamps/clothes pins		
Stands		
Gel stock (colour correction)		
AUDIO		
Microphones (wired or wireless or both as backup)		
Microphone cables		
Headphones		
Boom pole		
MISC		
Duct tape (gaffer tape if you have the budget)		
Pen/paper (for field notes)		
Personal Release Forms		
Video monitor (to check signal)		
Scripts		
Shot List		
Storyboard		

CD Filename: production.pdf

Production

The Director in the Classroom • Shot List

Project Title:

Shot	Int/Ext	Description

CD Filename: shotlist.pdf

The Director in the Classroom • Call Sheet

Weather: _____

_____   **CREW CALL:** _____   Date _____
Project Title

_____   **SHOOTING CALL:** _____   Day _____ of _____
Executive Producer

Scene #	Set	Bdgt	Hrs	Cast	Action/Desc.	Location
	Total:					

Cast/Extras	Characters	Time Required at Location

Props	Wardrobe	Special Notes

Transportation Notes	Cover Set	Emergency #'s

CD Filename: callsheet.pdf

The Director in the Classroom • Basic Call Sheet

Project Title: _____

Executive Producer: _____

Shooting Day _____

Shooting Date _____

Crew Call: _____

Shooting Call: _____

Estimate Finish: _____

Location: _____

Directions: _____

Scenes Scheduled:

Scene #	Scene Description	Estimate Hours

Crew

Roles	Name

Notes:

CD Filename: basiccall.pdf

The Director in the Classroom • Production Report

Project Title: _____   Day: _____

Executive Producer: _____   Date: _____

Crew Call	_____	Tape Time	_____
Shooting Call	_____	Previous	_____
First Shot	_____	Today	_____
Wrap	_____	Total	_____

Scenes Scheduled _____

HOURS

#		Budget	Actual	To Do	Reason if No

CD Filename: prodreport.pdf

The Director in the Classroom • Field Footage Log

Title:

Log Tape #:

Date Recorded:

Time	Scene	Take	Comment

CD Filename: footage.pdf

The Director in the Classroom • Work Timesheet

Name:	Project Title:	
Date:	Hours Worked:	Position:
Description of work completed:		
Date:	Hours Worked:	Position:
Description of work completed:		
Date:	Hours Worked:	Position:
Description of work completed:		
Date:	Hours Worked:	Position:
Description of work completed:		
Date:	Hours Worked:	Position:
Description of work completed:		

CD Filename: workheet.pdf

The Director in the Classroom • Edit Decision List

Project_____Date_____Page_____

_____

Tape	In		Out		Shot Description	Time
						TOTAL

CD Filename: edl.pdf

The Director in the Classroom • Personal Release

I, _____ give permission to _____ to photograph, videotape or otherwise record me for the purpose of using my likeness and voice for the student video production titled:

_____

Scheduled for shooting:

_____

I also understand that this production may be broadcast or distributed at the student producers' discretion, and may be seen on video, in theatres or on broadcast television and other media.

Signed _____

At _____

In the presence of:

_____
Signature

_____
Printed Name

_____
Address

_____
Student Producer

The Director in the Classroom • Permission to Use Copyrighted Material

I, _____, give permission

to _____ to use my (our)

copyrighted material(s) in the student video production titled:

_____

The materials to be used are:

_____

The student production shall use the materials only in the following manner:

_____

If required, the credit line shall read as follows:

_____

_____

Signed _____

At _____

In the presence of:

_____
Copyright Holder

_____
Student Producer

Post-Production

CD Filename: copyright.pdf

General Copyright Books
- Branscomb, A. W. (1994) Who Owns Information? From Privacy to Public Access. New York: Basic Books.
- Bruwelheide, J. H. (1995) The Copyright Primer for Librarians and Educators. (2nd Ed.) Chicago, IL: American Library Association.
- Goldstein, P. (1994) Copyright's Highway: From Gutenberg to the Celestial Jukebox. New York: Hill and Wang.
- Strong, W. S. (1993) The Copyright Book: A Practical Guide. (4th Ed.) Cambridge, MA: The MIT Press.

Online Copyright Resources
- Analysis of the Michigan Document Services Case
- http://arl.cni.org/scomm/copyright/mds.crews.html
- Consortium of College and University Media Centers Fair Use Guidelines for Educational Multimedia
- http://www-act.ucsd.edu/webad/fairuse.html

Copyright Act of 1976, as Amended
- http://www.law.cornell.edu:80/usc/17/overview.html

Copyright Clearance Center Online
- http://www.copyright.com

Copyright Directory
- http://www.mmwire.com/copyright/cresc.html

Copyright Website
- http://www.benedict.com

CREDO (Copyright Resources for Education Online)
- http://www.ilt.columbia.edu/projects/copyright/ ILTcopy0.html

Cyberspace Law for Non-Lawyers Online Course
- http://www.counsel.com/cyberspace

Intellectual Property Caucus of the Conference on College Composition and Communication
- http://www.Geocities.com/Athens/3375

Intellectual Property and the National Information Infrastructure (The White Paper)
- http://www.uspto.gov/web/ipnii

U.S. Copyright Office
- http://lcweb.loc.gov/copyright

Here is a brief overview of the basic equipment for filmmaking in the classroom. Detailed and up to date information on particular models and features may be found at: *<www.thedirectorintheclassroom.com>*.

ESSENTIALS
- A Camera
    - Digital Video (DV)
    - DV 8
    - Super VHS (S-VHS)
    - VHS
    - 8mm
    - Older formats include Betamax and 3/4"

- Editing Software
    - iMovie (Macintosh:) www.apple.com/imovie/
    - Final Cut Pro (Macintosh): www.apple.com/finalcutpro/
    - Premiere (Macintosh/Windows): www.adobe.com/products/ premiere/main.html
    - Videostream (Windows): www.videowave.com
    - Draco Casablanca System: www.draco.com

ENHANCEMENTS
- Tripod (to create steady shots)
- Things to move the camera (to create more exciting, moving, visual images)
    - Wheelchair
    - Swivel Chair
    - Grocery Cart
    - Skateboard
- Lights
    - Worklights
    - Floodlights
    - Lamps
    - Safety Gloves

- o Reflective Materials and Foam Core
  (to bounce light at subject)
- Sound
  - o Microphones
  - o Headsets

- Analog to Digital Converters (for importing analog footage like VHS and Hi8 into digital editing systems)
  - o Power R Directors Cut: http://sabre.forest.net/powerinc-24/index.cfm
  - o Dazzle's Hollywood: http://www.dazzle.com/products/hw_bridge_gut.html

EDUCATION

www.apple.com - Apple's homepage

www.apple.com/education/dv - Desktop Movies in Education

www.apple.com/education/k12/imagine/0204/miw/imovie/index.html - Production
Hints

www.atomiclearning.com - Free and Subscription Training

www.educationplanet.com - Educator approved resources/services

www.microsoft.com - Microsoft's homepage

www.griffin.multimedia.edu - Vancouver Film School

www.geocities.com/Hollywood/Highrise/1713/film.html#classroom - Filmmaking
Education

www.athensacademy.org/instruct/media_tech/reeves0.html - Use of computers in
the elementary and middle school classrooms

www.gse.uic.edu?cli/mathhtmls/math1video01big.html - Use of computers in the
elementary and middle school classrooms

http://loudon.k12.va.us./schools/littleriver/4class/four.htm - Distribution within
Schools

www.italian.nwu.edu/telenovela/telenovela.html - Italian Soap Opera

HARDWARE/SOFTWARE

www.videolink.ca - Canadian owned and operated desktop video and 3D animation
software and hardware dealer
– source for digital video, 2D/3D animation and display products—great
links

www.mh20.com - software allows beginners to professional musicians to create
their own music

www.ebay.com - great auction site for equipment, etc.

www.sony.com - hardware equipment

www.jvc.com - equipment

www.panasonic.com - equipment

www.skycrane.com - camera equipment

www.panasonic.com - hardware site

www.nomatica.com/video/gammevideo.htm - large listing of digital cameras cat-
egorized by maker, i.e. JVC, Panasonic, Thomson, Sony, etc.

www.alternatek.com/cameras.htm - Canadian source for digital video equipment

www.videoclipstream.org - source for video accessories

www.cantrek.com/shop/electronics.html - Shop Canada Online, digital video cameras, video cameras, digital cameras, camcorders, minidisks etc.

www.mandafilms.com - film/video equipment rentals

www.dvcentral.org - go to DV and Firewire Central 'cause they're the source for consumer digital video

FILM

www.filmfestivals.com - extensive site listing international film festivals with links to film festival sites around the world, plus festival chat room and festival search engine

www.moviesindepth.com/fest.htm - extensive listing of world-wide film festivals sorted alphabetically

PUBLICATIONS

www.macworld.zdnet.com - e-zine

www.alcanseek.com - search engine for publications for computer related subjects

www.cinemaspot.com/industry/magsjournals.htm - this site features publications that celebrate the art and science of film

SERVICES

www.on2.com - video compression pioneers

www.avid.com - Avid Technology, Inc. delivers the solutions that Make, Manage and Move Media™. As a recognized digital standard for media professionals—from video, audio and film to animation, special effects and streaming media

VIDEO PRODUCTION

www.rodan.asu.edu/~guy/video1.html & www.rodan.asu.edu/~guy/videoediting.html - comprehensive site presenting basic concepts of Desktop Video Production—gives step-by-step approach to the whole video production process. There's a video forum too.

www.dv.com - Video shooting information—comprehensive site featuring how-to's and great resources

www.cyberfilmschool.com/links/video.htm (# 1 site) This site features links to various video related sites on the web to teach everything about video production

www.videouniversity.com/ - all kinds of information about desktop video production and more—outstanding content, great links and resources

www.videomaker.com - Jam-packed with articles and online forums this site gives you the goods on making professional looking video—access their online archive, plus tons of videos and resources

SEARCH ENGINES

www.home.about.com - great search engine for film festivals, video equipment

www.webmovie.com - *WebMovie.com* is one of the most popular sites for film and video producers with 27,000 regular users performing thousands of daily searches to find the crews, equipment, facilities, services and technologies that they need for their productions

TECHNICAL INFORMATION

www.griffin.multimedia.edu/~mbrown/nav/index.html - Mike's Multimedia site dedicated to anyone who wants to setup and maintain a multimedia studio at home—very detailed

www.thetechnozone.com/videobuyerguide/videoediting-techtips.html - great links and information

www.desktopvideo.about.com - great site for desktop video related subjects, resources, links, free desktop video newsletter, chat, FAQ's, tips, news and cool links

.

.

Image Making

Visual Communication: Images with Messages
Paul Martin Lester/ 1999

Visual Language: Global Communication for the 21st Century
Robert E. Horn/ 1999

The Alphabet Versus the Goddess: The Conflict Between Word and Image
Leonard Schlain/1999

Visual Explanations: Images and Quantities, Evidence and Narrative
Edward R. Tufte/ 1997

Mapping Inner Space: Learning and Teaching Visual Mapping
Nancy Margulies/ 2001

Teaching Multiliteracies Across the Curriculum:
Changing Contexts of Text and Image in Classroom Practice
Len Unsworth/ 2001

Map It Out: Visual Tools for Thinking, Organizing, and Communicating.
Elisabeth H. Wiig / Carolyn C. Wilson/ 2000

A Field Guide to Using Visual Tools
David Hyerle/ 2000

Up and Out: Using Critical and Creative Thinking Skills to Enhance Learning
Andrew P. Johnston/ 1999

Strategies for Creative Problem Solving
H. Scott Fogler/ Steven LeBlanc/ 1994

The Ideal Problem Solver: A Guide for Improving Thinking,
    Learning, and Creativity
John D. Bransford / Barry S. Stein/ 1993

Use Both Sides of Your Brain
Tony Buzan/ 1991

Pre-Production

Using Video In the Classroom
L. Vangorp/ 2001

Global Scriptwriting
Ken Dancyger/ 2001

The New Scriptwriter's Journal
Mary Johnson/ 2000

Crafting Short Screenplays that Connect
Claudia H. Johnson/ 2000

The Visual Story: Seeing the Structure of Film, TV, and New Media
Bruce A. Block/ 2001

From Word to Image: Storyboarding and the Filmmaking Process
Marcie Begleiter/ 2001

Storyboards: Motion in Art, 2nd edition
Mark Simon/ 2000

The Storyboard for Film, TV, and Animation
John Hart/ 1998

Movie Worlds: Production Design in Film
Heidi Ludi/ Toni Ludi/ 2000

Art Direction for Film and Video
Robert Olson/ 1998

Creating Digital Content: A Video Production Guide for Web,
    Broadcast, and Cinema
John Rice/ Brian McKernan/ 2001

Basics of the Video Production Diary
Des Lyver/ 2000

Producing and Directing the Short Film and Video
Peter Rea / David K Irving/ 2000

The Digital Filmmaking Handbook
Ben Long / Sonja Schenk/ 2000

Production Management for Film and Video
Richard Gates/ 1999

Pre-Production Planning for Video, Film, and Multimedia
Steve R. Cartwright/ 1996

Film and Video Budget
Deke Simon/ 2001

Video Production Handbook, 3rd edition
Gerald Millerson/ 2001

The Computer Videomaker Handbook:
A Comprehensive Guide to Making Film, 2nd edition
Videomaker Inc. (Videomaker Magazine)/ 2001

The IFILM Digital Video Filmmakers Handbook
Maxie D. Collier/ 2000

Production

Shooting Digital Video
Jon Fauer/ 2001

Directing Film
Ken Russell/ 2000

Professional Cinematography for Cinematographers, Directors, and Videographers
Blain Brown/ 2001

Every Frame a Rembrandt: Art and Practice of Cinematography
Andrew Laszlo / Andrew Quicke/ 2000

Sound for Film and Television, 2nd edition
Tomlinson Holman/ 2001

Sound Person's Guide to Video
David Mellor/ 2000

Basics of Video Lighting, 2nd edition
Des Lyver / Graham Swainson/ 1999

Lighting for Television and Film
Gerald Millerson/ 2000

Post- Production

Digital Non-Linear Desktop Editing
Sonja Schenk/ 2001
The Technique of Film and Video Editing
Ken Dancyger/ 2001

Creative After Effects 5.0:
Animation, Visual Effects, and Motion Graphics Production for
    TV and Video
Angie Taylor/ 2001

Audio Post-Production in Video and Film
Tim Amyes/ 1999

Festivals/ Awards

And the Genie Goes To: Celebrating 50 Years of the Canadian Film Awards
Maria Topalovich/ 2000

Brave Films Wild Nights: 25 Years of Festival Fever (Toronto Film Festival)
Brian D. Johnson/ 2000

Directors Close Up:
Interviews with Directors Nominated for Best Film by the Directors Guild of America
Jeremy Kagan / Directors Guild of America/ 2000

Sundancing: Hanging Out and Listening at America's Most Important Film Festival
John Anderson/ 2000

Film Theory

How Movies Work
Bruce F. Kawin/ 2001

Digital Filmmaking: The Changing Art and Craft of Making Motion Pictures
Thomas A. Ohanian / Michael E. Phillips/ 2000

Documenting Ourselves: Film, Video, and Culture
Sharon R. Sherman/ 1998

The Oxford Guide to Film Studies
John Hill/ Pamela Church Gibson/ 1998

Understanding Movies
Louis Giannetti/ Jim Leach/ 1996

Film History

A History of Experimental Film and Video
AI Rees/ 1999

A Short History of the Movies
Gerald Mast/ Bruce F. Kawin/ 1996

Cultural Theory

Media and Literacy: Learning in an Electronic Age: Issues, Ideas, and Teaching Strategies
Dennis M. Adams / Mary Hamm/ 2000

The Triumph of Narrative: Storytelling in the Age of Mass Culture
Robert Fulford/ 1999

Essential Mc Luhan
Marshall Mc Luhan / Eric Mc Luhan / Frank Zingrone/ 1996

Reference Material

Job Descriptions for Film and Video: Responsibilities and Duties
  for the Cinematic Craft Category
William E. Hines/ 1998

Key Concepts in Cinema Studies
Susan Hayward/ 1996

The Complete Film Dictionary
Ira Konigsberg/ 1989

The Director in the Classroom
How Filmmaking Inspires Learning

Workshops
&
Presentations
by
Nikos Theodosakis

For information on workshops and presentations please contact:
Nikos Theodosakis
The Director in the Classroom
687 Main Street
Penticton, British Columbia V2A 5C9
Toll Free: 1-866-696-7777
nikos@thedirectorintheclassroom.com

and to view a video clip of Nikos in action, visit our web site at:
www.thedirectorintheclassroom.com.

Nikos Theodosakis lives in Canada and travels internationally consulting, producing workshops and speaking on the topic of integrating filmmaking into the classroom.

His workshops for educators invite participants to become filmmakers and experience the technologies and thinking processes involved in multimedia production through the creation of their own video. Participants work in teams, using Digital Video cameras and computer based editing systems to make their own movies. They learn how to plan, shoot, and edit their ideas and then transfer them onto videocassette and as QuickTime movies ready for the World Wide Web.

From initial idea to final presentation, participants explore how storyboards, pitching, scripts, planning, filming and editing contribute to the development of visual, oral and written presentation skills. They explore how filmmaking can enrich learning, build community, bring social issues alive and create projects that promote higher order thinking skills, self esteem and creativity. And then they eat popcorn.